AGGRESSION MANAGEMENT WORKBOOK WITH C

Anger Management ESSENTIALS

Anita Avedian
Licensed Marriage and Family Therapist

Dedication

To my mother and my late father, who never gave up their support of my endeavors. I love you both very much.

Acknowledgements

Many thanks to all those who have helped author and edit the Anger Management Essentials workbook, especially the ever evolving and wonderful Anger Management 818 team.

First, I thank all of my contributing authors, who researched important material and helped with creating worksheets designed to improve people's skills in dealing with anger. It would have been a challenge for me to be able to develop more than 50 lesson plans on my own, so their help in coming up with fresh and practical material was invaluable. The contributing authors are: Sylvia Cary, MFT; Ingrid Caswell, MFT Intern; Angela Andikyan, MFT Intern; Molly Lyda, MFT; Rachel Thomassian, MFT; and Farnaz Toutouni.

As they say, it takes a village to write a book. Without my editors, Sylvia Cary, MFT, and Ingrid Caswell, MFT Intern, my extra pairs of eyes, you might be finding typos, grammatical errors, and worksheets that don't make sense. I also want to thank Edmon Artinyan, and Jennifer Liff, for some extra editorial assists. I appreciate all of their efforts to make Anger Management Essentials a professional contribution to the field.

I couldn't have done any of this without the love and support of my parents. They have always encouraged me to pursue my dreams and not give up.

Many thanks to my mentor in the field, Corie Skolnick, MFT. I have always seen her as someone who has looked out for my best interests, and has provided me with so much support and guidance. When there have been opportunities in the field, she would encourage me to pursue them, because she gets satisfaction from seeing other people succeed. I've seen her give unconditionally to the people around her. This is one of the reasons why so many colleagues and friends think highly of her, as I do.

I want to acknowledge Laurie Brumfield, who asked me years ago if I wanted to start an anger management program with her. Without the partnership, I probably would not have been as involved within the anger management field.

There's also Brad Klimovitch and Dr. Kathie Mathis for helping me start the California Association of Anger Management Providers, which is currently the California Chapter of the National Anger Management Association. A special thank you to Rich Pfeiffer, President of the National Anger Management Association (NAMA), for his guidance in the anger management field.

And finally, I want to acknowledge the ideas of George Anderson which have influenced the writing of some sections of this book.

ISBN-13:978-0615964003

Published by Anger Management Essentials Publishing

www.AngerManagementEssentials.com

Book cover design: T.L. Price Freelance
Book cover photo: Morguefile.com

Table of Contents

Foreword by

Hagop Akiskal, MD (AΩA)

In an era when depression and bipolar disorder have become a part of our daily vocabulary as respectable disorders of mind and brain, another pervasive emotional disorder is relatively neglected. This book by Anita Avedian focuses on a disorder of relational emotional life, which not only can cause damage to interpersonal relationships, but can also lead to violent acts.

A perusal of the literature for vocabulary describing anger is actually quite rich: Ill humor, temper, irascibility (easily flying off the handle), choleric (which actually is one of the four classic temperaments), irritation, vexation, fury, outrage or indignation (anger provoked by what is perceived as unfair treatment), distemper (which is a canine contagious viral illness, but sometimes seen in humans who may become unpredictably violent). But isn't it true that our species is capable of the most sublime emotions like dedication, devotion and love, yet capable of hatred, enmity, genocide, even killing in the name of ideology?

Certainly, alcohol and drugs, and certain unbearable life circumstances can escalate anger to violent extremes in both men and women. However, this monograph is **not** about these extremes of violent anger, but about the emotion in the daily lives of men and women, which nonetheless can impair, even damage, marital relationships and family life.

Treatment in a group setting, which includes both men and women, is an ideal setting to work through the dark side of emotion in daily life.

This book is comprehensive, easily accessible to a general readership. It is not doctrinaire, and covers the most commonly utilized psychotherapeutic approaches, thereby succeeding in its aim to be relevant and useful for a wide range of the adult population confronted with anger in certain phases of their lives and psychohistory.

HAGOP SOUREN AKISKAL, MD (AΩA)

h.c. (Lisbon, Aristotle U),

DLFAPA, FACPsych, MRCPsych(hon,UK)

Distinguished Professor of Psychiatry

University of California at San Diego

Director of International Mood Center

Welcome to Anger Management Essentials

Starting an anger management program can be an exciting, yet intimidating, journey to initiate. You may be reading this workbook due to the request of the courts, attorneys, the workplace, or for personal reasons. We have found that there may be some hesitation or resistance to participating, with the hopes of completing the workbook quickly without considering the necessity or benefit of practicing the skills learned. Most people have found the content within this workbook to be very beneficial and as a result, they embraced the ideas herein and found themselves motivated to change. If you are skeptical and apprehensive, we hope your experience will result similarly.

We commend you for recognizing the need to change and improve how you deal with anger. Welcome to taking the steps necessary to achieve a happier and more fulfilling life. Thank you for choosing the Anger Management Essentials workbook. We truly enjoy helping people grow and experience breakthroughs that create positive changes in their lives. We hope that you will find this experience to be a rewarding one.

What to Expect - To receive the maximum benefit of an anger management workbook, we encourage you to practice the skills learned. The sooner you practice these skills, the better you will be at incorporating them into your life. If you are using this workbook in an anger management program, we recommend that you inform your facilitator about your experience of testing the skills. By doing so, your counselor will be able to coach you through using them properly.

Please note that one does not improve by simply learning the skills. To foster change in your behavior, it is essential to apply the skills to your daily life. As the creators of this workbook, we will do our part in teaching and guiding, however your commitment to practicing and making necessary changes is vital to your success. Similar to weight loss, you can learn about it but unless you exercise and eat healthier, you won't achieve your goal.

Improving your anger management skills begins with the following:

1- Commitment to making a change. *This includes completing the lessons within this workbook, and practicing them in your daily life.*

2- Being open. *This includes understanding yourself better, recognizing how you feel inside, noticing signals from your body, and receiving feedback from others.*

3- Being proactive. *This includes planning ahead to avoid anger triggers and anger inducing situations.*

The key components of the Anger Management Essentials Program include:

1- Understanding Anger
2- Communication and Listening Skills
3- Emotional Intelligence and Empathy
4- Developing Healthy Relationships and Boundaries. Understanding Co-dependency
5- Stress Management
6- The Use of Cognitive Behavioral Tools to Improve Thoughts and Beliefs
7- Anger Management
8- Letting Go and Forgiveness

Check-In Format for Anger Management Classes

1. State the situation in a few (three or four) sentences.

2. How did you feel?

3. What was your behavioral reaction?

4. What would you like from the group? To share only? Or to share and receive feedback?

Example 1:

1. State the situation in a few (three or four) sentences. *I interviewed for a job. The employer said he'd contact me in two days, but by the second day he hadn't called. So I called him. His secretary answered and he wouldn't take my call.*

2. How did you feel? *I felt angry and ignored.*

3. What was your behavioral reaction? *I called back four more times that afternoon and left four messages with his secretary for him to call me. Then I called a fifth time and left a message that I didn't want the stupid job any more.*

4. What would you like from the group? To share only? Or share and receive feedback? *I'd like to know how you guys think I could have handled it differently.*

Example 2:

1. State the situation in a few (3 or 4) sentences. *My girlfriend told me she thinks we should "take a break" and see other people.*

2. How did you feel? *I felt sad, scared and humiliated.*

3. What was your behavioral reaction? *I ripped up the photo of her I had in my wallet and threw it in her face. I screamed at her and called her a whore. I smashed her favorite vase on the floor, walked out of her house and slammed the door.*

4. What would you like from the group? To share only? Or share and receive feedback? *I just want to talk about how hard it is to always have these relationships end the same way. I'm so tired of it and I just feel like I'll never find a good person to be with.*

Understanding Anger

What is anger?

Anger is a feeling -- a powerful but perfectly normal human emotion. Some may think that anger is a behavior, but it is not; aggression is the behavior. We can feel the emotion of anger yet choose to express it in different ways (passively, assertively, aggressively, etc.).

Anger is also a signal. It serves us by providing important information about ourselves and our needs in relation to others. For example, if a friend arrived half an hour late to meet you for lunch, and you felt upset about her being late, then your anger served as a signal: punctuality is an important value to you.

Finally, anger is energy. As energy, it provides us with the drive and determination to take action, as well as to cope with difficult situations. Fortunately, it is within our power to decide how to channel, or direct, the energy of anger in more productive ways.

How Anger Works Physiologically

Your body works in a very specific way when you feel anger. The first thing that happens is that neurotransmitter chemicals located in your brain called *catecholamines* release, causing an influx of energy in your body that can last up to several minutes. During this time, several physical symptoms are noticeable, such as rapid breathing, higher blood pressure, accelerated heart rate, and muscle tension. In addition, blood flows to the limbs in preparation for physical action. Many people experience their attention narrowing to the target of their anger and sometimes see red. Shortly thereafter, hormones such as adrenaline and non-adrenaline, and additional brain neurotransmitters, are released, triggering a higher state of arousal. With this burst of physical energy, you're ready to take immediate action; you're ready to fight.

Given this information, it is easy to see how quickly you can lose control of your anger. However, it is quite possible to learn how to regain control, simply by understanding how the amygdala and the prefrontal cortex work. The amygdala is an almond-shaped mass in your brain that handles emotion -- it is related to survival. It gets us reacting before we can really think about the situation. The prefrontal cortex, on the other hand, located just behind your forehead, handles judgment. It is responsible for regulating your behavior and making choices. The left prefrontal cortex, in particular, can switch off your emotions, keeping things under control. Basically, we are wired to react at times before we can really think about the consequences of our actions. Therefore, the more you learn ways to give your prefrontal cortex the upper hand over your amygdala, the more control you will have in response to your anger.

The Wind-Down Phase of Anger

Anger can last a very long time -- for hours, and sometimes even for days -- and it can take time to relax after an angry episode. That is why there is a wind-down phase. During this phase, we begin to relax back towards our natural resting state. Usually at this time, the target of our anger is no longer accessible or an immediate threat. Keep in mind that this cool-down period takes time, and our anger threshold is lower than usual during this phase. What this means is that we are more likely to get very angry in response to minor irritations that normally would not bother us.

In addition, it is important to know that high levels of arousal significantly decrease your ability to concentrate. Since you will feel lingering arousal during the wind-down phase, it may be difficult to clearly remember the details of an angry outburst.

Anger as a Secondary Emotion

Though we may not realize it, we feel other emotions before anger. These preceding emotions are called primary emotions. Some examples of primary emotions are: fear, anxiety, shame, sadness, frustration, guilt, disappointment, worry, jealousy, embarrassment, hurt, helplessness, and insecurity.

Here's an example: Let's say that someone is tailgating you while you're driving. The driver is putting you at risk, and you feel threatened. Anger is one of the two feelings that will come up. Fear is the other feeling. Which feeling, then, is the primary emotion: anger or fear? Fear. Fear is the natural, first-level emotion in response to feeling threatened. Anger is the secondary, protective response. Without anger, all you have is fear in the face of danger. Anger, after all, is the energy of action and helps you decide what to do.

A Healthy Anger Response

Anger has its benefits. At its most basic level of functioning, it can be used to protect ourselves and our loved ones. Anger can improve relationships by opening up lines of communication. In addition, it can help us feel stronger and healthier.

Knowing that anger itself is a healthy human emotion, how can we respond to challenging situations using a healthy anger response? Let's go back to the earlier example of tailgating to demonstrate. If someone is tailgaiting you and your safety feels endangered, try this on for size: simply slow down to a speed that will cause the driver to pass you. If an accident happens, there will be less damage because of the slower speed.

This is a healthy option from the standpoint of learning about anger. For one, it gives you a way of communicating to tailgaters that you don't like what they're doing, and it further shows them that you are not going to be intimidated into driving faster or dangerously to get out of their way. In addition, you are expressing your need for safety without exhibiting aggression.

We need plenty of options for dealing with our anger. The above is just one healthy way of dealing with a difficult situation. Some tips to follow:

1. Identify why you are angry.
2. Decide which issue to address.
3. Prioritize what's most important to you.
4. Create an action plan that will be most beneficial.

A final point is that anger will arise from time to time, and when it does, just remember: you have the power to choose how to respond to your own anger. Each day, you have the opportunity to practice expressing your anger in more and more healthy ways.

ANGER, AGGRESSION and RAGE: What's the Difference?

Why do people sometimes say, "I'm getting angry," but not "I'm getting enraged?" What's the difference between anger and rage? And where does aggression come into the conversation? We often use the words anger, aggression, and rage interchangeably, but actually they have many differences. Understanding the differences amongst anger, aggression and rage is essential to developing healthy psychological habits and clearing away unhealthy ones. Although they do share *some* qualities in common, many of the following characteristics of anger, aggression and rage differ from one another:

- What they are a response to
- How long they take to build up and subside
- Their physical effects
- Their proportionality to the provocation
- Whom they assign responsibility to
- What their intention is
- What their effect on others' feelings is
- What they result in

First, let's look at how these principles define **ANGER**:

RESPONSE TO... Anger is a feeling. It's a **natural, healthy emotional response to injury or intrusion.** True anger can be a response to hurt, frustration, disappointment or threat (real or imagined). It's a signal, or alarm, that something is not right, that we do not feel okay about what we're observing. The gift of anger is that it motivates and gives us energy and confidence to make valuable changes in our lives. Expressing anger is all about the controlled notification that we feel threatened in some way. It's communicated assertively, without hysterics: "I'm angry, here's why, and here's what I need...." Most importantly, anger is about something that is happening in the present moment, or close to it.

TIME... Anger builds slowly, possibly over hours or days. It subsides quickly, once the provocation ends, usually within 30 seconds to two minutes. It's brief and then let go of with a sense of pleasure.

PHYSICAL EFFECTS... Anger is dealt with in the parasympathetic nervous system – the same system responsible for "rest-and-digest" or "feed-and-breed" activities like salivating, digesting food, sleeping, or having sex. Think of these functions as pleasurable ones that occur when the body is at rest. When we are experiencing true anger, our breathing deepens, our vision becomes more focused, we have a warm feeling in the skin, our movements become smoother, and our memory becomes clear.

PROPORTIONALITY TO PROVOCATION… Anger is about something happening in the present moment, and therefore its expression is proportional to the event.

ASSIGNED RESPONSIBILITY… Someone experiencing true anger takes responsibility for the feeling. "When **I** heard that you gave the promotion to your newly-hired boyfriend, **I** thought all my years of hard work at this company are not valued, and **I'm** feeling angry." So, "When this happens, **I** feel angry," not "**You** are making me feel angry."

Anger comes from acceptance - as opposed to denial - that what has happened has happened. Be careful not confuse "acceptance" with "like". We often confuse the two because we only accept what we like!

INTENTION… Expressing healthy anger is about connecting. It seeks to get the listener's attention, inform, engage, and communicate. Also, anger demands no specific response. It lets the chips fall where they may without needing to control the outcome. All responses to healthily expressed anger are considered valuable information in terms of making decisions about the future of the relationship.

EFFECT ON OTHERS' FEELINGS… Anger draws out others' feelings. "I" statements create space and safety for the other person to engage in healthy communication without defensiveness. "It wasn't my intention to make you feel undervalued here. I could see how it might feel that way to you. The truth is I value you very much. In fact, two positions have opened up simultaneously. You're skipping a level and will be promoted above my boyfriend."

RESULTS IN… Healthy anger results in feeling genuine and truly self-expressed. At its best, anger draws people closer together and enables them to get their needs met. At the very least, it helps us to set boundaries with others. If your boss says, "You're right, I don't value your efforts at this company," that's essential information you can use to set a boundary for yourself. Maybe you decide you want to get a different job where you are appreciated.

Now let's look at **how AGGRESSION compares to anger**, using the same principles.

RESPONSE TO… **Aggression** is a behavior. It is an abusive way of behaving verbally, emotionally or physically. Like anger, aggression is a response to a perceived insult, injustice or wrong-doing, however, aggression looks very different from anger. This is due to the difference in the way a person *perceives* another person's intentions. Let's look at an example of aggression - as opposed to anger - in response to a perceived threat. While an actor is shooting a scene in a movie, the lighting director is walking around behind the camera, within the actor's line of sight. The actor becomes distracted and has to stop the scene. It's too difficult to concentrate on everything he must do to perform well (remember lines, step into the light at the right moment, pretend the camera isn't there, etc.) with the lighting director distracting him as well. If the actor perceives that the lighting director is intentionally being insulting and disrespectful or trying to undermine his performance, the actor will be triggered for aggression. He might become verbally and emotionally abusive or attack the director physically. (Whereas with healthy anger, the actor would not be focused on the other's intent, but rather on his own feelings, and would be able to say, "Please don't walk around during shooting. It's too distracting for me.")

ASSIGNED RESPONSIBILITY… Aggression blames the other for one's feelings. It perceives the other's actions as intentionally insulting or disrespectful.

TIME… As you can imagine, aggression is impulsive, and therefore comes on quickly. And because it's caused by large amounts of cortisol and adrenaline being dumped into the body's system, it can take quite a while to subside – hours, even days – while the body struggles to process the chemical overload.

PHYSICAL EFFECTS… Aggression is activated in the sympathetic ("fight-or-flight") nervous system, in the old brain known as the amygdala. This system is responsible for the stimulation of activities that prepare the body for action. When there is a threat, the brain sends a signal to the pituitary gland, and cortisol and adrenaline are released in great quantity. When these hit the bloodstream, the following occur: the heart rate increases; the body shakes; we get tunnel vision; we experience hearing loss; and our digestion slows (this makes sense because digestion is controlled by the parasympathetic nervous system, which cannot operate when the sympathetic nervous system is in control.)

Why do our bodies do this? In caveman times, you were okay if you could fight it or run away from it. -The stronger your sympathetic nervous system, the better. We no longer face this sort of threat in modern society, but our bodies have not changed. If we look at aggressive driving, John Doe is sitting in his car feeling very entitled to his little piece of the road and the way that he wants to drive. If someone is encroaching on John's space or making decisions that aren't in John's best interest, he feels threatened. "Road rage" occurs when John's body prepares to face a threat in a situation where action is not possible. For someone about to run a marathon, it's very helpful for heart rate and adrenaline levels to shoot up, but if John's sitting in a traffic jam with nowhere to go, it's a recipe for disaster.

PROPORTIONALITY TO PROVOCATION… Aggression is over-the-top and disproportional to the event.

INTENTION… Aggression seeks to cause emotional or physical harm. It wants to frighten, punish, or manipulate the other.

EFFECT ON OTHERS' FEELINGS… Others' feelings are trampled.

RESULTS IN... Aggression is very isolating because people learn to tip-toe around you, or they choose to end their relationships with you altogether. Aggression can result in serious problems at home, work, and with the law. It is also responsible for medical problems such as headaches, digestion issues, insomnia, anxiety, depression, high blood pressure, skin problems (eczema), heart attack, and stroke.

So, how does rage measure up? As mentioned earlier, the terms "anger", "aggression" and "rage" are often used interchangeably, but for the purpose of distinguishing them, it's easiest to think of rage as a math problem, where unexpressed anger and aggression are present together in their most intense forms: **(ANGER + AGGRESSION) x 10 = RAGE**

<u>RAGE</u>

RESPONSE TO... Rage is a response to a threat to pride, status, or dignity. The roots of rage are in childhood, when a kid was helpless against abusive adults or older kids. When something in the present triggers an old memory, the reaction is to the memory, not to the present event. Thus the behavior is frightening, unexpected and seemingly inappropriate. Rage is not a feeling, so much as it is an emergency defense activated in the fight-or-flight, sympathetic nervous system. When rage is triggered, "conflict recognition" areas in the emotional brain – or amygdala - are stimulated, and they lose contact with the executive part of the prefrontal cortex, which is responsible for rational decision-making. Rage can be activated by an external cue, like the murder of a loved one. Or rage can erupt after multiple "stuffing's" of unexpressed anger and perceived disrespect. When we are enraged, we believe that someone is deliberately trying to incite us and we need to "even the score".

Rage can be a response to shame, abandonment, exposure, power and control, and disinhibition. Let's look at each one more closely.

Shame: a feeling of inadequacy and an inability to justify one's existence. (Guilt says, "I did something bad. Stop doing it." Shame says, "I am bad. I should not exist.") Shame is an intolerable feeling, and rage is an escape from it. But, of course, rage is a future cause of shame, and this perpetuates the shame-rage cycle.

Abandonment: Being 'left' or 'left out' is devastating for a child, and many people carry this wound into adulthood. When the abandonment goes unhealed, even a temporary separation from a partner who leaves to go to work can trigger a reactive rage. For some, a difference of opinion can be a rage trigger.

Exposure: This is when an event uncovers evidence that something the rager has been denying is in fact true.

Power and control: Because rage intimidates others, the rager acquires power and control, which become a re-enforcement for more rage. This is most evident in domestic abuse.

Disinhibition: A rager experiences an adrenaline high. Adrenaline decreases inhibition.

TIME... People say, "I'm getting angry...", but not "I'm getting enraged...." That's because there is no buildup or "getting there" with rage. In a fight-or-flight reaction, potent chemicals are dumped into the bloodstream that highjack the body and mind immediately. Rage is instant. Once adrenaline hits the bloodstream, its effects last for 1-2 hours. Unless you actively practice it, muscle tension cannot be reversed quickly. Rage persists long after the provocation ends.

PHYSICAL EFFECTS... Rage causes muscle tension, pounding heart, rapid and shallow breathing, pale skin, tunnel vision, and severely compromised - if not total blackout of - memory. This is where the expression 'blind rage' comes from. Enraged people may be capable of doing things that seem physically impossible. Adrenal surge increases physical strength, raises endurance levels, and dulls the pain sensation. After a rage, the rager often does not remember it, which aids in denial.

PROPORTIONALITY TO PROVOCATION... Although rage may be triggered by a present event, the enraged reaction is over-the-top and disproportional to the situation. This is because rage is about something that happened a long time ago that has not been healed from, and that's why it's seemingly excessive and inappropriate. This is what is meant by the expression "If it's hysterical, it's historical."

ASSIGNED RESPONSIBILITY... Rage blames the other and perceives the other's actions as intentionally insulting or disrespectful.

INTENTION... Rage wants to control and silence the other.

EFFECT ON OTHERS' FEELINGS... Rage obliterates others' feelings. Often others decide to cut-off from ragers.

RESULTS IN... Loss of jobs, freedom, and relationships. Beliefs and principles the rager has developed in life are inaccessible. Previous agreements are abandoned. History of bonding, attachment, good will or shared pleasures are denied.

If rage happens more than once or twice a year, it will dominate the dynamics of any relationship. Rage can become an addiction, because it works. If you are a frightening, intimidating person, people back off and you get what you want. Loss of self: the rager is temporarily without personality, a defensive entity at war with the world.

SUMMARY

ANGER	AGGRESSION	RAGE
Feeling	Behavior	Extreme Behavior
Non-Violent	Possibly Violent	Violent
Healthy	Unhealthy	Unhealthy
Controlled	Out of Control	Out of Control
Clear Thinking	Incoherent Thinking	Blackout of Thought
Engaging	Trampling	Obliterating
Safe	Unsafe	Possibly Lethal
Quick and released with pleasure	Long-lasting and held onto with resentment	Long-lasting and held onto with resentment
Accepts what has happened	Denies what has happened	Denies what has happened

HELP! WHAT CAN WE DO ABOUT ANGER?

"CLAIM IT. TAME IT. AIM IT."

Claiming: Accepting (opposite of denying) the legitimacy of one's self-protective impulses and recognizing the effects of anger in the body.

Taming: Shifting the self-protective impulses from the sympathetic or rage system to the parasympathetic or social engagement system. This usually means doing some bodywork. Taming also means developing the capacity to hold anger long enough to shape it into a humane response.

Aiming: Channeling the energy of anger through the social engagement system to remove the cause for the anger. It is movement toward a constructive goal. 'Stewing' with anger is not aiming! Perhaps aiming will include protest, but complaining in a way that makes it clear that the complainer is not prepared to participate in a solution is called whining, and this is also not aiming.

Use the TALKING BOUNDARY

SENSORY DATA (Observable Behavior):

*When I saw...

*When I heard...

THOUGHTS (Always speak from the "I" position.):

*What I made up about that is...

*What I believe about that is...

*What that has triggered from my past is...

EMOTIONS (Emotions are generated from our thoughts):

*and about that I am feeling...

IN THE FUTURE (Vulnerable Request):

*What I would like/prefer is...

-Pia Mellody

10 TIPS FOR ANGER

1- Think before you speak.
2- Once you're calm, express your anger.
3- Get some exercise.
4- Take a timeout.
5- Identify possible solutions.
6- Stick with "I" statements.
7- Don't hold a grudge.
8- Use humor to release tension.
9- Practice relaxation skills.
10- Know when to seek help.

WHAT CAN WE DO ABOUT AGGRESSION?

CLASSICAL CONDITIONING (Behavioral Therapy)

Desensitization is a type of conditioning that changes the relationship between a stimulus and a response. Pair social criticism (honking, cursing, and yelling) with relaxing behavior (singing). This extinguishes the relationship between social criticism and aggression.

REMOVE ALCOHOL and OTHER DRUGS

Alcohol, stimulants, anabolic steroids, and marijuana impair perception and alter mood states. During the later stages of dependency, alcohol causes a decrease in levels of the neurotransmitter serotonin. Studies of rodents and nonhuman primates show that when serotonin is unavailable or its transmission is impeded, animals become aggressive and impulsive. Rats with low serotonin levels will attack and kill other rodents.

GROUP THERAPY

Aggression is a learned coping skill for people with a history of abuse and neglect. Children decide between ages of 8 and 14 not to get close to or be hurt by anyone ever again. For example, a father beats son with a belt when the father is drunk. The son decides at age 12 this will not happen again. When the father comes after him with a belt, the son physically attacks him. This survival mechanism follows the boy into adulthood. In group therapy, the adult son's family dynamics are reenacted, and he may dare the therapist to confront him. When he observes that the therapist and other groups members don't respond to him as his father did, the group becomes a healing mode of recovery.

COGNITIVE THERAPY

This approach addresses how people's underlying assumptions about themselves, the world, and their future, as well as their automatic thoughts, trigger feelings. For example, the core belief that the world is a dangerous place is shifted to a more helpful, moderate, and realistic one.

RELAXATION THERAPY

Progressive Muscle Relaxation (PMR), Meditation, Guided Imagery, Paced Respiration and Deep Breathing all strengthen the relaxation response.

INSIGHT ORIENTED THERAPY

This is effective when aggression is part of an early developmental theme such as abandonment. Attachment rage develops when a person had a rejecting parent who used threat and withdrawal to discipline. Insight oriented therapy helps the person connect the dots from past childhood to present adulthood. Neglect and abuse issues seem to be right-brain oriented; Insight oriented therapy stimulates the right brain.

WHAT CAN WE DO ABOUT RAGE?

Decrease sympathetic tone and increase parasympathetic tone through breathing exercises, stretching, Pilates, and yoga. Increase fine-motor control to strengthen the connection between the executive areas of the cortex and the limbic system through: bodywork, Pilates, yoga, martial arts, and Brain Gym® exercises.

MEDICATION

When there is a psychiatric disorder, such as depression, present with the rage, medication can prevent rage outbursts. Antidepressants (namely selective serotonin reuptake inhibitors, or SSRIs), mood stabilizers like lithium and anticonvulsants, and antipsychotics increase activity in the prefrontal cortex, which reduces impulsive aggression.

SOBER COMPANION

The primary duty of a sober companion is to keep a rageaholic emotionally sober. They provide on-call or round-the-clock care and/or accompany the recovering rageaholic during activities that stress them. Companions use diet, exercise, massage, distraction, meditation, acupuncture, prayer and affirmation, and chiropractic adjustments. Sober companion treatment usually lasts for 30 days or longer. Ideally, a companion's presence in a recovering person's life will decrease as the person's ability to confront family, work, and legal issues without relapse is proven.

DECREASE SHAME

Shame is the engine of denial, which fuels rage.

IDENTIFY DENIAL

Denial is not accepting that something that has actually happened has happened. Ongoing denial is never stable because the actions and statements of others will threaten it. When this happens, fight-or-flight dynamics and rage erupt. After rage subsides, denial reforms, perhaps strengthened by shame about the outburst. Other people affected by the rage learn not to challenge the denial. This is a self-perpetuating process.

IDENTIFY RESENTMENTS

Denial and resentment are related. Denial is the disbelief that something that has happened has happened. Resentment is the belief that something that happened should not have. The most justifiable reason for this position is the belief that it happened through the ill will of somebody else (and should be reversed by some imaginary judge). Resentment is a psychological defense used to hide an unmet need or desire that is seemingly too painful to acknowledge. To dissolve resentment, it is necessary to discover and admit what one really wants or wanted.

A Path to Recovery

There are many consequences of anger. Place a check mark next to the negative consequences of anger that resonate with you. If you are in recovery from anger, place a check mark next to the positive consequences that apply to you.

Negative Consequences of Anger	**Positive Consequences of Recovery (or calm)**
ANGRY	CALM
Suspicion	Trusting
Resentment	Forgiveness / Letting Go
Insecurity	Confidence
Complacency	Self- Examination
Need to Control	Positive surrender
Reactionary	Responsive
Accusing	Empathic
Assuming	Facts
Impulsivity	Patience
Win/Lose – Competitiveness	Win-Win – Cooperativeness
Overwhelm	Manage stress - or time management
Aggressive or Passive Aggressive Communication Styles	Assertive Communication Style
Black/White Thinking	Grey Thinking
Blurring of Boundaries	Healthy Boundaries
Codependency	Interdependency

Review the challenges of the negative consequences.

How can you work towards the positive consequences?

How would your life be different?

Advantages to Working on My Anger

In order to become a more calm person, it's first important to assess your level of motivation, and reasons for wanting to change, otherwise, you may find yourself feeling resistant to the information in this workbook.

To start, list your reasons for wanting to change below. Usually, people want to change because there was an incident that led to a loss of a job, or a relationship, or some trouble with the law. What are your reasons for wanting to work on your anger now?

1- ______________________________

2- ______________________________

3- ______________________________

4- ______________________________

On a scale of 1-10, 10 being very motivated, and 1 being not at all, how would you rate your level of motivation to work on your anger?

1 2 3 4 5 6 7 8 9 10

On a scale of 1-10, 10 being very willing, and 1 being not willing at all, how willing are you to change your reactions when you're upset?

1 2 3 4 5 6 7 8 9 10

Many clients enroll in an anger management program—either because they have to, or because of an incident. Working on your anger is an ongoing process. One strategy to help you stay motivated is to remind yourself of all the reasons why you want to be a calmer and more understanding person, and reduce aggressive behavior.

Some common reasons people want to work on their anger include:

1- My anger scares my partner, and I don't want to scare people.

2- I've lost several jobs because of my anger. It's time I make a change.

3- Being more trusting and understanding makes things so much easier.

4- I want to sleep better at nights.

5- My health and blood pressure will improve.

Make a list of advantages to being calmer and more understanding in the section below:

1- ______________________________

2- ______________________________

3- ______________________________

4- ______________________________

5- ______________________________

6- ______________________________

7- ______________________________

8- ______________________________

Add to this list when you think of additional advantages. It helps to have this in your notes app on your phone, so that the list is available for you to read at your discretion.

The purpose of reading your list of advantages on a daily basis for the next month is to help you get into the mindset of having a new focus. The days you read this list, you may have a better attitude towards those around you, and life in general.

Anger Manifestations at Different Levels

Anger is sneaky and you may not even realize you're upset until certain symptoms appear. The following lists provides various indications that anger is manifesting itself at numerous levels: physical, emotional, behavioral, and cognitive. Familiarizing yourself with the symptoms below will assist you in managing your anger, because the sooner you *recognize* them popping up, the sooner you can effectively *deal* with them. On the other hand, if you don't address them at the early stages, you may find yourself muttering "I go from 0 to 10 in a second," and you're left feeling helpless and doubting that you'll ever change. Use the empty spaces below to add symptoms you experience that are not already listed.

PHYSICAL
High or low blood pressure
Eye twitching
Heart rate increase
Nausea
Upset stomach
Fatigue
Shaky hands
Chest pain
Tense and tight muscles
Jaw clenching
Stiff neck
Teeth grinding
Difficulty sleeping
Headache
Hair standing up

EMOTIONAL
Distrust
Depression
Irritability
Hopelessness
Low self-esteem
Impatience
Negativity
Anxiety
Overwhelm
Apathy
Short temperedness
Confusion/ confliction
Fear
Resistance
Suspicion

BEHAVIORAL
Restlessness
Short responses
Over or under eating
Increased drinking
Road rage
Changes in sexual behavior
Inattention
Distancing self from others
Isolating
Forgetfulness
Smoking and/or drugs
Indecisiveness
Increased use of profanity
Unkempt/ Lack of hygiene
Neglecting home and office environment

COGNITIVE
"What is she thinking? How could she not know that?"
"Oh no, I don't think I can handle this."
"He's out to get me. I just know it."
"I won't succeed."
"I won't get through this."
"I can't do this."
"She did this on purpose."
"No one is helping."
"He's ruining my life. It's all his fault."
"She's so selfish. She only cares about herself."
"She's very sneaky. She knows what she's doing."
"He should know. I've told him many times."
"She's the one who needs to change. Not me." "This is too much."
"I need help."

lain Sources of Anger: Anger Turned Outward versus Inward

rstand anger, it is helpful to identify the two common sources of anger, threat and frustration.

1- Threat –We feel threatened when we think our personal power is at stake.
2- Frustration –We feel frustrated when our needs go unmet.

When we feel threatened or frustrated, we also feel helpless or hurt, which oftentimes leads to a state of Anxiety. Anxiety is an intolerable state, and we do anything we can to relieve the tension. What we do depends on the following situations:

a. If we feel that we deserve the situation, we could begin to feel guilt, and as a result, blame ourselves. This is where we turn inward and become angry at ourselves. Consequently, this leads to more anxiety and further feelings of hurt and helplessness.
b. If we don't feel that we deserve the situation, we may express our anger outwardly. This could include blaming others, shouting, physically harming others, or breaking things.
c. Some healthy ways to express our feelings of anxiety could be assertive communication, deep breathing, or physical exercise. It would be difficult to learn from the experience if we don't share our feelings and find healthy means to release the tension.
d. It is common for some to turn their anger outward, and others inward. When anger is turned outward, we risk harming others and losing our support system. When anger is turned inward, we harm ourselves, and we could become depressed.
e. Let's look at some examples of anger turned outward versus inward:

Anger Turned Outward	**Anger Turned Inward**
Express anger verbally - yell	Feeling upset
Manipulate	Substance use
Control others	Feeling unhappy
Hostility	Feeling hurt
Clenched fists in other's presence	Feeling guilt
Insulting remarks	Feeling inferior
Intimidation	Low self-esteem
Threats	Isolation
Verbal Abuse	Feeling violated
Rage	Feeling helpless/ powerless
Tease	Resentment
Damage to property	Overeating

The idea is to work through and resolve the anger. Don't ignore it.

Taking action: doing something about the problem/ situation

A good start is to learn to express feelings respectfully and appropriately, in a way where someone can hear you.

Another possibility is to learn problem solving skills and work through the various triggers and stressors in your life.

Working through your anger

If you're not ready to take action such as communicating your concerns with the direct source, and you cannot change the situation, then the next best thing is to take care of yourself and your anger.

1- Talk to someone you can trust, and release your concerns.
2- Physical exercise - this is a great way to discharge some negative emotions.
3- Journal writing - explore the source of your anger. Understand it so that you can be supportive to yourself.
4- Meditate - ground yourself, and take care of yourself.

Whatever you do, don't ignore your anger. Talk to the source, change the situation, or take care of yourself.

Keeping Track of My Anger

The purpose of the Anger Log is to track situations where you became angry. Tracking your anger can help put things into perspective after a challenging event occurs, potentially helping you prevent such situations in the future. Let's review a sample log.

1. What was the situation? *I was waiting in line at the supermarket. Another register opened, and the person standing behind me rushed to go there.*

2. How did you handle it? *I told him, "Didn't you see me standing before you? You need to ask me if I wanted to go first."*

3. What did you want to happen? *I wanted the guy to know that he was being inconsiderate, and for him to learn a lesson.*

4. Were you able to get what you wanted from the way it was handled? *Yes* (*No*)

5. What thoughts did you have during the situation? *He's so inconsiderate and thinks he can get away with it. What if I was the type of person who couldn't speak up for myself. Guys like him need to learn a lesson.*

6. How did you feel during the situation? *I felt taken advantage of and angry.*

7. What was the outcome of the situation? *He yelled at me, and said to mind my own business. The cops came and I got into trouble with the law; now I have to take courses.*

8. Did you get physically violent? *Yes* (*No*)

9. Did anyone get hurt physically? *Yes* (*No*) *Emotionally?* (*Yes*) *No* If yes, how? *He threatened me by saying he's calling the cops. He must have felt threatened as well.*

10. How did you feel after your reaction? *Angry at first, however, fearful that my wife was going to get upset at me for handling the situation poorly.*

11. What could you have done differently? *Asserting to the person, "Excuse me, I believe I was here first. Do you mind if I go before you?"*

12. What are some thoughts that could have helped you achieve a better outcome?
    - *a.* *It's not a big deal. It's only a few minutes of waiting.*
    - *b.* *It's not up to me to teach everyone a lesson.*
    - *c.* *People have differences; the more understanding I am, the more patient I am.* *

The last question is the most important aspect of this worksheet. When you are aware of both destructive and constructive thought patterns, then you have the power to choose your thoughts, and ultimately make better choices in handling difficult situations.*

Keeping Track of My Anger

1. What was the situation?____

____

2. How did you handle it? ____

____

3. What did you want to happen? ____________________________________

____

4. Were you able to get what you wanted from the way it was handled? Yes No Somewhat

5. What thoughts did you have during the situation? _________________________

____

6. How did you feel during the situation? ________________________________

7. What was the outcome of the situation? _______________________________

____

8. Did you get physically violent? Yes No

9. Did anyone get hurt physically? Yes No Emotionally? Yes No If yes, how?

____

10. How did you feel after your reaction? ________________________________

11. What could you have done differently? _______________________________

____

12. What are some thoughts that could have helped you achieve a better outcome?
    1. ____
    2. ____
    3. ____

Keeping track of your angry encounters helps you identify your destructive patterns. Awareness is the first step towards change.

CALL TO ACTION: For better success in managing your anger, complete the questions thoroughly following each upsetting episode.

Keeping Track of My Anger

1. What was the situation?____

2. How did you handle it? ____

3. What did you want to happen? ____

4. Were you able to get what you wanted from the way it was handled? Yes No Somewhat

5. What thoughts did you have during the situation? ____

6. How did you feel during the situation? ____________________________

7. What was the outcome of the situation? ____

8. Did you get physically violent? Yes No

9. Did anyone get hurt physically? Yes No Emotionally? Yes No If yes, how? ____________________________

10. How did you feel after your reaction? ____________________________

11. What could you have done differently? ____

12. What are some thoughts that could have helped you achieve a better outcome?
    1. ____________________________
    2. ____________________________
    3. ____________________________

Keeping track of your angry encounters helps you identify your destructive patterns. Awareness is the first step towards change.

CALL TO ACTION: For better success in managing your anger, complete the questions thoroughly following each upsetting episode.

The Course of Anger

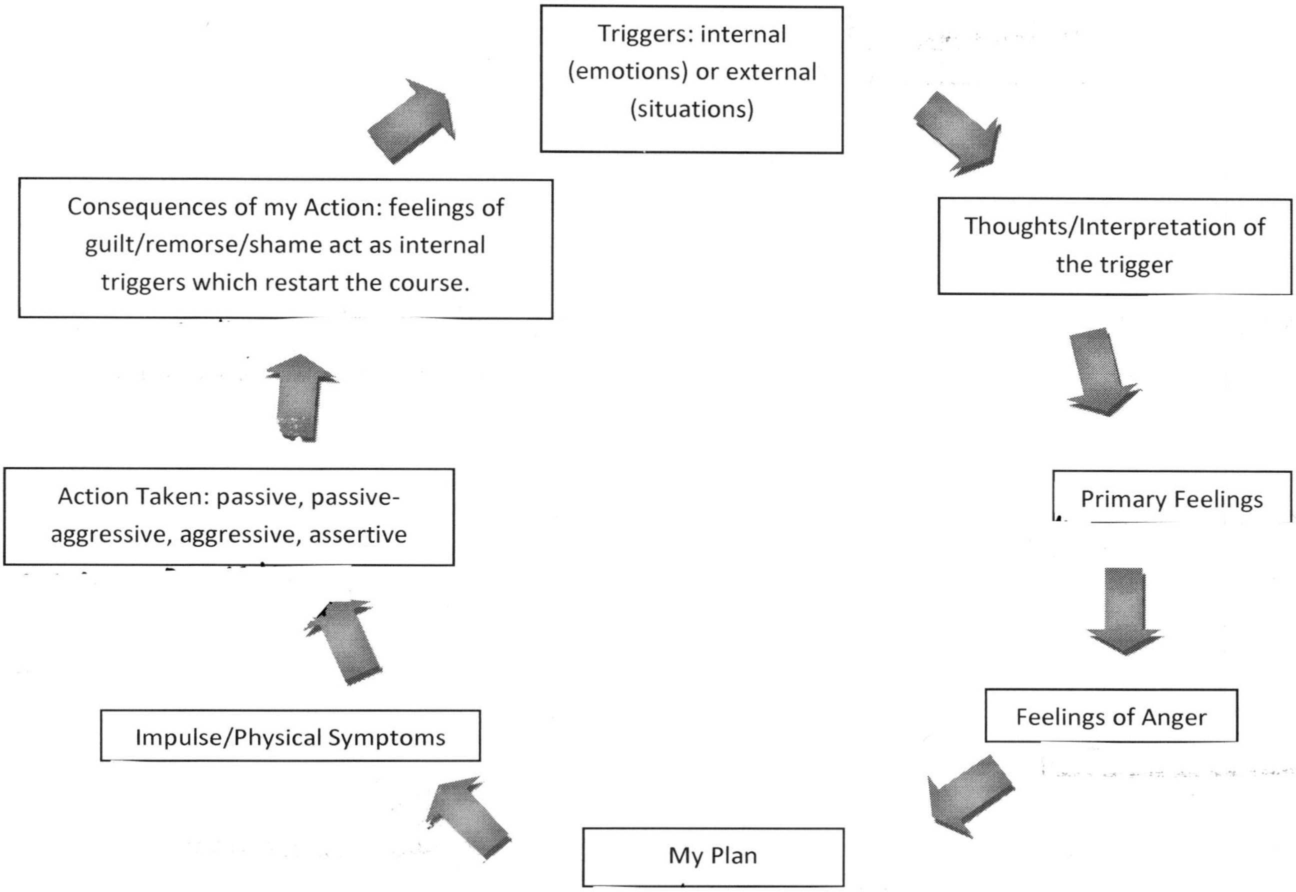

Trigger: I'm waiting for a parking space with my turn signal on, and someone takes my spot.

Thoughts/Interpretation: This person knew I was waiting and disrespected me by taking my space.

Primary Feelings: Stress and anxiety because I'm running late; a little helpless not knowing how to respond.

Feelings of Anger: Angry and frustrated.

My Plan: To get revenge: "I'll show him!" I will either tell him off or key his car.

Impulse/Physical Symptoms: Adrenaline pumping, shallow breathing, and heart racing.

Action Taken: Aggressive – I honk my horn and yell at the driver for being inconsiderate.

Consequence: Feelings of shame and guilt that I handled the situation poorly. My child has witnessed my yelling and I have modeled improper behavior for him.

Internal Trigger – The guilty feeling may trigger the course to begin again.

Breaking the Course of Anger

Now that we understand that the course of anger includes several components, let's take a closer look at each element, and identify where we can throw a wrench in the works, so to speak, to break the pattern. The left column lists the individual components of the course from the previous page, and the right column identifies the skills or tools that are the remedies, or countermeasures, for the items on the left. These skills and tools are explained in detail throughout this workbook and should be used to counter the negative effects of triggers.

Event/ Trigger	• Problem solve through triggers. • Avoid triggers.
Thoughts/ Interpretations of the Trigger	• Countering thoughts • Alternative ways of interpreting the situation
Feelings/ Emotions	• Identify both primary and secondary emotions, and embrace them. • Express feelings appropriately.
Plan	• Alternative options • Check with others for a better plan.
Impulsive/Physical Symptoms	• Tension release • Deep breathing • Exercise
Action Taken	• Behavioral change - assert yourself • Walk away if necessary.
Feelings of Guilt/ Remorse	• Learn to sit with/tolerate your emotions. • Process emotions - write in a journal or talk to someone.

Not only is it easier to counter the initial effects of a trigger, but efforts made earlier in the journey will yield more productive outcomes than actions taken at later stages. In some cases, especially when the course reaches its end stages, it may become impossible to break the trigger pattern.

Anger Triggering Thoughts

Simply put, a trigger is anything that stimulates a reaction. Triggers can be as obvious as cars honking on the freeway or as subtle as someone turning her head to look at you. Triggers bring back past memories that provoke fear, rage, or lust in us. When triggered, we lose our awareness of the present and become gripped by the object of our attention. We read into and react to the slightest thing. In these states, our survival instincts in the "reptilian brain" hijack our higher brain functions and spark a fight, flight or freeze response.

Triggered emotions can feel negative or positive. Arguments as well as sexual attraction can set the nervous system on high alert creating a "rush," or a feeling of being high. Such reactivity undermines autonomy, or self-control. People with serious past physical or emotional trauma will likely experience triggers as unconscious defense mechanisms and they will be seen from the outside as knee-jerk reactions; the person will be viewed as having a "hair-trigger" personality. "If it's hysterical, it's historical" is a common 12-Step saying. When we are emotionally triggered, there is usually unprocessed trauma from the past clouding our perspective. Past memories inform all our present-day interpretations.

The more we are in relation with others, the more we are triggered. We all have emotional triggers. Triggers trick us into believing that there is only one way to respond to them. They greatly limit our behavioral options. If we can become aware of what our triggers are, we can gain control over our reactions and make better choices for ourselves. We don't have to blow up and blame the world for our struggles or throw caution to the wind and indulge in self-gratification.

Below is a list of trigger thoughts associated with feelings of anger. They are grouped into five categories: Magnification, Labeling, Entitlement, Mindreading, and Assumptions. As you read through the list, place a check mark next to the ones that sound familiar. Perhaps you've had these thoughts during angry episodes.

Magnification- *Focusing on the negative aspects of the situation.*

____ 1. You never do what I ask.

____ 2. You're always doing your own thing and not paying attention to me.

____ 3. You're never there for me.

____ 4. You're always controlling and telling me what to do.

____ 5. People don't try to get to know me.

Labeling – *Using words to label people or situations.*

_____ 1. You are acting ridiculously right now.

_____ 2. You are being very manipulative.

_____ 3. She's a gold digger, that's why she wants me to take her out to the nice restaurants.

_____ 4. He's a pig. He's going to mistreat me because of his career.

_____ 5. You always have to be right. You're not going to listen so what does it matter anyway.

Entitlement – *Just because you want something, you believe that you should have it.*

_____ 1. This is my seat. I always sit here in class.

_____ 2. I paid her money for this workshop. She better stick around to answer my questions.

_____ 3. He has to attend to me no matter what I say. He's my waiter.

_____ 4. She's my girlfriend; she has to cater to me.

_____ 5. He's customer service. He has to help me.

Mindreading- *Assuming you know what someone is thinking or feeling without checking in with them.*

_____ 1. You're doing this intentionally just to annoy me.

_____ 2. You oppose everything I say. Why can't you just side with me for once?

_____ 3. I know you don't really care. You're just saying that to appease me.

_____ 4. I know you don't really want to go.

_____ 5. You think I don't realize what you're really thinking of me?

Assumptions- *When you apply special meaning to someone's behavior.*

_____ 1. If you really loved me, you would have offered to go with me.

_____ 2. You didn't call me because you completely forgot about me.

_____ 3. If you really wanted to be working here, you would follow my requests.

_____ 4. If you really cared about customers, you would do as I ask.

_____ 5. You obviously don't respect me because you always flake.

What are your emotional triggers? Write out a list and commit it to memory to strengthen your mindfulness in the moment. Common triggers include: predictable stressors like business meetings, deadlines, due dates; interactions with certain people; or anniversaries of significant events. When you feel triggered, determine the inciting incident and add it to your list!

The next time you're triggered, name the trigger out loud. "Someone honked at me, and I feel triggered." Say it over and over and then release a deep breath. If it's appropriate to respond, do so. But first try to recover emotional sobriety. This is one of the most challenging life adjustments you can make, so be patient with yourself!

Some of my more intense triggers are:

1.______________________________

2. ______________________________

3. ______________________________

4. ______________________________

5. ______________________________

6. ______________________________

7. ______________________________

8. ______________________________

9. ______________________________

10. ______________________________

Countering Thoughts for Anger

Countering thoughts is an important tool to help increase positive emotions. Cognitive theory suggests that our thoughts directly impact our emotions. Thus, if our thoughts are irrational or negative, then most likely we will feel unnecessarily upset. The purpose of this exercise is to help you perceive situations in a more realistic and neutral manner.

Angry Thoughts	Countering Thoughts
He did that on purpose. I'll show him.	1) How do I know he did that intentionally? Perhaps he didn't realize that it was going to affect me. 2) Even if I show him, he may have no idea what lesson I'm trying to teach him. 3) I often don't trust people, so this may be another situation where I'm misinterpreting his actions.
I shouldn't have to explain myself.	1) Though I would like for my partner to read my mind, I know that's not possible. 2) It is my own challenge to express my feelings properly. My partner is saying that he/she doesn't understand; it is my responsibility to explain further. 3) The purpose of communication is to clarify.
I cannot trust people.	1) Who said? Though I have felt betrayed in the past, it does not mean that I will be betrayed again. 2) I have trusted my friend and not gotten hurt. 3) I have a habit of looking for reasons to not trust people. If I look hard enough, I will most likely find something.
She caused me to be angry.	1) No one caused me to be angry. I am angry because of my own interpretations of the event. 2) It sounds like I want to be blaming my emotions on someone else, when I know it has to do with my own expectations. 3) She didn't force me to be angry or say that I needed to get angry. It's a choice.

Exercise: Counter Your Angry Thoughts

Instructions: List your own angry thoughts in the first column, and try to counter your thoughts in the second column (at least 2 countering thoughts per angry thought).

Angry Thoughts	**Countering Thoughts**

*To get the most value from this tool, we encourage you to counter your upsetting thoughts daily. If you practice this skill consistently, you will notice positive changes in your thinking habits. The benefit of your initial hard work is that, over time, countering your thoughts will become automatic and will come naturally to you.

Anger Triggering Situations and Some Pet-Peeves

There are many situations that trigger anger or frustration. Review the following list to identify how much the trigger would upset you. Rate as follows:

0- No trigger 1- Mild trigger 2- Moderate trigger 3- Severe trigger

General Situations

1. Cell phone users with loud voices in public places
2. Elevator conversations that are too personal
3. Elevator conversations to show off, name drop or "perform" for others
4. Petty thefts, such as newspaper, plant or umbrella stolen from front door
5. Smoking in non-smoking areas
6. Someone cutting ahead of you in a line
7. People who won't take "No" for an answer
8. Pushy sales people
9. Passive-aggressives who manipulate, control or twist things to get their way
10. Loud gum chewing and cracking
11. People who don't carry their own weight at home, work, socially, or in the community
12. Getting advice from people who know nothing about your situation
13. People who talk too much
14. People who abuse animals or children
15. People who lie
16. People who gossip
17. People who complain about things that no one can change, like the wind
18. People who keep making the same mistakes even after being corrected
19. At the deli or bakery counter, the employee skips your number
20. You're at a meeting, and the leader keeps calling on others rather than you
21. People who think they have you fooled when you see right through them
22. People who blame others for their own lack of success
23. People who complete your sentences for you
24. People who have talents but refuse to do anything with them and complain about being "bored" with life
25. People who don't want to do what it takes to achieve a goal
26. Receiving phone calls from telemarketers

Social Media

1. People who refuse to learn about new technology
2. People who don't know what they don't know and won't learn
3. People who think Facebook is real life and refer to things they read there
4. People who post fabricated information about others on social media
5. Posting or tagging a picture of you without your consent

6. You see pictures of your friends getting together without having invited you
7. You notice through social media that your ex is in another relationship
8. People who disclose too much on social media (TMI)
9. Cat fishing- people who make a fake profile

Driving/ Car Related

1. Tailgating
2. Aggressive or show-off driving
3. Traffic congestion when you're late for a meeting or appointment
4. You're waiting for a parking spot and somebody else zips in and takes it
5. People who drive in the no passing lane or on shoulder to get ahead of you
6. Inconsiderate drivers who refuse to let somebody else go first
7. People who talk on the phone while driving even where it's illegal to do so
8. Drivers who pull in ahead of you, then jam on their breaks causing you to slam on your brakes, almost causing an accident
9. A driver texting at a red light doesn't notice when the light turns green
10. Women putting on make-up while driving
11. Men shaving while driving
12. People eating while driving
13. Drivers turning to talk to people in the back seat and not watching the road
14. Drivers going fast in residential areas where there are kids and joggers
15. The car behind you honks for you to pull out into traffic when they can't see what you can see -- which is that there's a huge truck coming up on your left
16. Being a passenger of a car with the driver being careless or reckless

Financial

1. Identity theft
2. Losing a wallet, cell phone, credit card, etc.
3. Being ripped-off in any way
4. Out with friends who don't contribute enough cash to pay the bill and tip
5. Nickel-and-dime fees-- such as bank fees, ATM fees, fine-print fees, phone fees
6. Getting a parking ticket when you are only two minutes late to the meter
7. Getting home from the market and some items you need are missing because the checker and bagger were too busy talking to pay attention
8. People who abuse the time that they are being paid for at work by talking, gossiping, complaining, taking too long for lunch, and not getting the job done
9. People who envy what others have but don't take the necessary actions to achieve the same for themselves
10. "Tip included" automatically when the service is poor
11. Price goes up on an item
12. Your spouse is spending money that is not in the budget

13. People set up splitting the bill evenly when one has ordered a lobster tail and alcohol while another has only ordered a salad

Relationships

1. People who are mean to children or animals
2. People who are toxic, so you feel worse, not better, when you are around them
3. People who are ambivalent about being with you but won't say anything
4. People who talk about others behind their backs
5. People who flake
6. People who are petty
7. People who don't keep their word
8. People who don't take care of their health and surroundings
9. People who don't pull their own weight in a relationship
10. Women who don't understand men and don't bother to observe and learn
11. Men who don't understand women and don't bother to observe and learn
12. People who have "hidden agendas" in their dealings with you
13. Anyone who doesn't fulfill a duty, responsibility or promise and ignores it
14. Having to deal with the consequences of a bad relationship: separations, divorce, custody battles, financial squabbles, pain
15. Spouse is taking their time when there is a time restraint
16. Infidelity

Parenting

1. Not putting the safety and welfare of one's own children first
2. Not attending to "red flags" such as children having "problems" in school with their behavior or grades
3. Dealing with your parental feelings when your child does not make a sports team, dance team, etc.
4. Dealing with the fact that your child is not getting along with his/her peers
5. You don't like your children's friends
6. You don't like your children's friends' parents
7. Parents who are too rigid or impatient with their kids
8. Parents who are not honest with their kids or lie in front of them
9. Divorced parents who say bad things about their exes
10. Parents who swear around their kids, then are shocked when their kids repeat the bad words at school or in public
11. Over-pushing kids to excel
12. Letting kids run wild
13. Enabling kids
14. Parents who yell at a small child or a dog in public place in mean way
15. Overprotective parents
16. Parents who ignore their children frequently

Recognize Anger and YOU

When it comes to anger, we commonly don't realize how we get from one to ten so quickly. We tend to focus on what others do rather than on our reactions. Have you ever thought about what hurts you so much and why? What physically happens when you experience certain emotions? Often we are so busy being angry that we neglect to understand what is happening.

The following exercise will help you recognize your anger and how it impacts you. Welcome to the first step of anger recognition!

A. List one feeling that is difficult for you to tolerate, i.e. hurt, disrespect, betrayal, or disappointment

____

____

B. Identify a time you experienced this feeling when it was difficult to tolerate. What do you remember experiencing physically-- sweaty palms? racing heart? dry mouth? chest pain? Rate each symptom on a scale of 1 to 10 according to its level of intensity. For example, if you recall experiencing a racing heart, and it was quite intense, line a. could read, "Racing Heart - 8."

a. ________________
b. ________________
c. ________________
d. ________________
e. ________________

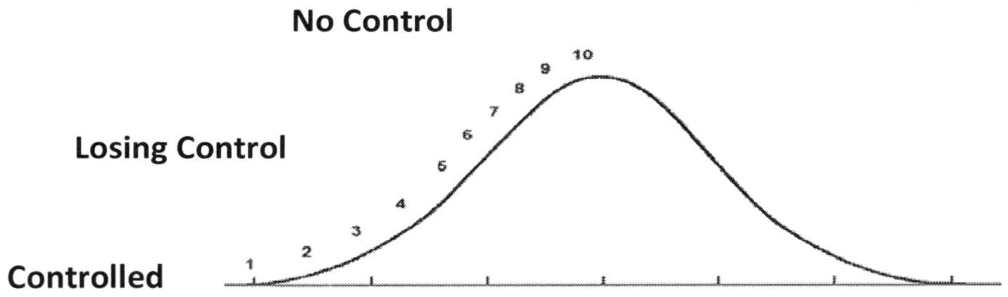

C. List the *behaviors* and/or *actions* you took upon experiencing physical symptoms, i.e. attacked verbally or physically, used harsher tone or sarcasm, became vindictive, or gave silent treatment.

a. ________________
b. ________________
c. ________________
d. ________________
e. ________________

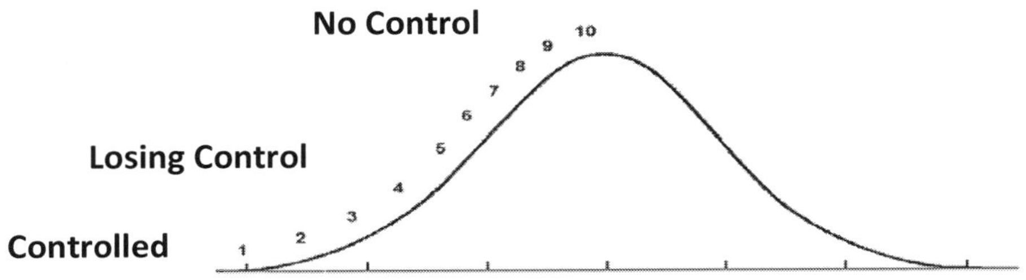

D. List events in your life that triggered this difficult emotion.

1. ____
   ____

2. ____
   ____

3. ____
   ____

E. List actions that might prevent it from happening again.

1. ____
   ____

2. ____
   ____

3. ____
   ____

Identifying the triggers that result in difficult feelings, physical symptoms, and accompanying behaviors, prevent you from losing control. The earlier you stop anger in its tracks, the easier it is to manage it. Continue to rate your levels of emotions and physical reactions in the upcoming weeks, and notice improvement with your anger.

Quick Tips for Taming Your Anger

Anger management clients often ask for quick tips that they can pull out of their back pockets at a moment's notice when they are triggered for anger. We live in a fast-paced world; it's normal to want immediate solutions to painful problems. The reality is that our unhealthy ways of dealing with anger have been *years* in the making – they were modeled for us in childhood by our caregivers and reinforced in all of our adult relationships. Obviously, it will take more than an afternoon to undo our destructive habits and learn to prevent anger by becoming more trusting and empathic of others, shifting our distorted perceptions, and communicating our needs effectively. In the short term, however, here are some gems that can buy you some time and peace of mind as you work on your deeper issues over the long term:

1- **Change the scene:** When things get heated, sometimes it's best to leave the situation. This helps shift your focus as well as your frame of mind. It provides the opportunity to reflect rather than to escalate.

2- **Take a walk**: Walking helps in several ways. When we walk, our bodies release chemicals called endorphins that have a calming effect on the body. Endorphins also reduce our pain perception. In addition, the continuous, cross-lateral (right-left) movement of arms and legs improves mood and alertness by stimulating both sides of the brain at the same time.

3- **Count to ten:** Counting disrupts emotion. Emotion is managed in the right hemisphere of the brain while logic is managed in the left hemisphere (theory originated by Roger W. Sperry). When you engage the left side of your brain in order to count, the right, emotional brain is disengaged. The act of counting also shifts your attention away from your angry thoughts.

   a. Another technique is to wear an **eye-patch** over one eye. This is an NLP (Neuro-Linguistic Programming) technique used to reduce feelings of tension. It can shut down the dominance of the right, emotional brain and help us to stay in logic. For some, covering the right eye produces this effect; for others, the left must be covered. To see which eye works for you, try this: Looking straight ahead and keeping both eyes open, think of a person or situation that bothers you. Cover your right eye for 10-20 seconds. Does this change the intensity of your emotion? Cover your left eye for 10-20 seconds. Assess whether your level of upset was decreased by covering your right or left eye. If you aren't sure, try again, and pay close attention to the intensity of your upset.

4- **Breathe with intention:** Consciously breathe very deeply for at least 3-4 minutes. Be sure to breathe into your diaphragm and not your chest. To assess whether you're breathing into your diaphragm, place one hand on your belly and the other on your chest. As you breathe in, your belly should fill with air, forcing your hand to move forward. If, however, when you breathe in, the hand on your chest rises, this means you are shallow breathing, which prolongs anxiety. Deep breathing into the belly/diaphragm relaxes the body.

   a. **Additional tip:** Count while breathing in and out: Inhale for a count of 4 seconds. Exhale for 8 seconds. This triggers the parasympathetic nervous system, which governs relaxation.

5- **Write:** Writing is a safe way to express and release uncomfortable emotions.

   a. **Journal Writing:** There are many styles of journaling and there is no "right" or "wrong" way to do it. Some people use free-style writing to simply identify their thoughts and feelings or to release extreme emotions that may not be safe or constructive to express to an actual person. A more structured method is to break up a journal entry into three parts. Part 1: Release your anger or frustration by writing about how it felt and how you behaved. This might seem destructive, but getting your thoughts *down on paper* and *out of you* is actually very healing. Part 2: Process and reflect. Ask and answer questions such as, "What does this mean about me?" and "What were my underlying thoughts that caused me to act this way?" Part 3: Set goals and make an action plan. How would I like to shift my behavior? How would that shift benefit my relationship? What is my plan for making this shift? How will I deal with obstacles along the way to changing my habits?

   b. **Write a Letter:** Write a letter to someone you're upset with. This is NOT a letter that you will send. (It's best to write on paper or in a Word document and not in an email, since accidentally hitting "send" would potentially ruin your effort to calm yourself.) Say everything you wish to say in the letter. Although it may seem strange, the act of simply writing the letter can help tremendously in recovering from upset. It is a cathartic experience that allows the unedited child in us to have a voice without negative consequences.

6- **Thought stopping** – Angry feelings are intensified by ruminating – reviewing thoughts over and over again. To interrupt this destructive thinking process, say out loud in a firm, authoritative voice, "Stop!" Imagine a big, red stop sign, or envision the upsetting event shrinking or floating away. Replace the upsetting thought with a pleasant one. Have a pleasant thought ready to pull out at a moment's notice.

7- **Helpful, positive self-talk –** Review a list of affirmations and positive self-talk statements. When you redirect your attention to the positive aspects of your life, you invite more pleasant feelings. Anger creates a lot of negative energy in your body; it is up to you to veer your attention toward affirmations and statements that are healing. For example: "At the core of all anger is a need that is not being fulfilled." - Marshall B. Rosenberg. Or "My anger is temporary; I'm not feeling heard right now, but when I calm down, I will be able to understand this situation better."

8- **Tension releasing –** Use stress balls to discharge anger tension. Anger manifests physically, and tension-releasing exercises help your body to let go of non-productive energy. They create relaxation and decrease the likelihood of angry outbursts.

   a. **Progressive muscle relaxation** - relax your muscles with this two-step process. First, systematically tense a particular muscle group in your body, such as your neck and shoulders, for a count of 5 seconds. Next, release the tension, and notice how soft and heavy your muscles feel. Do this for arms, hands, legs and feet. Repeat the cycle 3 times. This exercise lowers your overall tension and stress level.

9- **Tune in to your physical feelings –** Instead of running from your feeling, turn your attention towards it. This will lead you to feel more grounded. Tip: Use your senses to try to identify what the feeling looks like, including its color, shape and size. How heavy is it? What does it smell like? Does it have a texture? Where does it sit in your body? For example: you may feel a heavy block of black steel that smells of metal sitting in your chest area. Bring the feeling to life.

10- **Talk to someone you trust** – Call someone safe and supportive. This person is usually a good listener and offers helpful feedback. Tell them you'd like a few minutes to talk through a situation that is upsetting you. Be sure to not wear out your support system, and only call when it's truly important.

11- **Practice relaxation skills –** In addition to the breathing exercises and tension releasing described above, you can also use visualization and meditation to increase relaxation:

   a. **Visualization** involves imagining yourself in a relaxing environment, such as at the beach, with the sun's rays warming you.

   b. **Meditation** is the practice of watching your thoughts come and go without reacting to them. Find a quiet place to sit, or do a walking meditation in a familiar neighborhood or around a track where you don't have to pay close attention to your route. Meditation is a very grounding exercise, whether you do it for a minute or an hour.

12- **Listen to music** – Your favorite music can relax and put you in a better mood.

13- **Exercise** – Physical activity releases anger. Take out your anger on your bike or the pavement while you're running. As mentioned before, this releases endorphins and lifts your mood.

14- **Use humor** – Watch a funny movie or TV show. Learn to laugh at yourself.

NOTE: Although it may be helpful for some, be mindful that hitting punching bags or other objects can increase adrenaline and thus reinforce violence in others.

Additional techniques (your counselor may or may not be familiar with these):

1- **Hands folded with right thumb over left thumb** - NLP 4th generation. Activate the left hemisphere.
2- **Thought Field Therapy (TFT) / Emotional Freedom Technique (EFT)** – tapping on meridian points with a certain algorithm.

Anger Management Tips for the Long Haul

Often we want quick tips on how to get rid of our anger. Unfortunately, the work required to manage anger is more involved than that. The main focus of an anger management program is *prevention,* so that one has more manageable ways of dealing with feelings of anger and the desire to act out aggressively. One thing to focus on is the area of your "unmet needs" otherwise the anger will resurface. The more you understand your own anger, the more you will be able to communicate your wants and needs to those around you.

Helpful Tips in General

1. **Keep track of your anger –** When you want to make a change in any behavior, it is helpful to identify your patterns and the triggers to the behavior. This way you can either avoid the triggers or problem-solve through them. Start keeping a log of your angry moments to identify patterns. Some examples of triggers include being tired, hungry, or not feeling heard.

2. **How relevant is your anger?** Sometimes we get triggered and become upset when the situation doesn't really call for it. For example, on a scale of 1-10 (10 being very angry) if a person interrupts you while you're talking, and you go to an 8, where will you go if your girlfriend cheats on you?

3. **Anger as a protective emotion** – we usually feel angry in an effort to protect ourselves from a more painful emotion. Rather than covering the unwanted emotions, face them and work towards accepting and embracing them.

4. **Pay attention to your thoughts** - When you are upset, your thoughts will "sound" different to you. You may even notice the thoughts before you feel the emotions. These thoughts may be statements involving unrealistic expectations, angry thoughts such as, "He did it on purpose," "She's taking too long," "He needs to see it my way," or "Of course he's going to side with her; he always does."

5. **Set healthy boundaries -** Setting appropriate boundaries with yourself and others is essential to fostering healthy relationships. If you don't have good boundaries with yourself, then how can you have good boundaries with others? Make sure you are taking care of yourself and not overwhelming yourself by constantly putting others' needs before your own.

6. **Communicate assertively** - When you keep your disappointment or frustration to yourself, people around you will not know that something is bothering you, and thus they will not do anything to help. Keeping things to yourself can also lead to feeling resentful. Sometimes we *show* we are upset, but we don't actually *say* it, or say why.

This can confuse people around us. Be clear in communicating what's bothering you, and ask for what you want. Refrain from communicating aggressively.

7. **Check your expectations –** We are bound to be disappointed when we set unrealistic expectations of those around us. In place of saying, "You should," state "I would like." This technique will help you become more realistic and accepting. For example, "I would really like it if you would take me out for dinner on my birthday."

8. **Deal with your anger at its earlier stages -** Don't wait until you can't control your anger. When you notice your anger is around a 5 on a scale of 1-10, start working to reduce it. Meaning, if someone says or does something bothersome, communicate that to them in a respectful way. Or journal through your frustrations. It's easier to work with your anger at its manageable stages rather than waiting until it's too late.

9. **Take responsibility -** Many times we blame others when we are upset. It is up to you to take care of yourself, and ask for the type of support you want. It is your choice to eat healthy, work out, and schedule fun activities. If this is difficult for you, and you often blame others for your unhappiness, then it would help to work on issues surrounding co-dependency. For example, do you ever catch yourself saying, "You made me angry?"

10. **Be fair -** If you want to be heard and have your needs met, it's important to reciprocate. Negotiate when needed. Not all the decisions have to go your way.

It takes practice and effort to think more calmly, and to refrain from aggressive behavior. However, with all this effort, we may still slip and yell, or react inappropriately. In case this does happen, here are some suggestions:

1. **Show understanding -** If you did blow up at someone, or you were aggressive with them, try apologizing and share your understanding about how your behavior impacted them. For example, instead of saying "I'm sorry," say, "I can see how my yelling at you was scary. I'm sorry for placing you in an uncomfortable position."

2. **Be forgiving -** Holding onto anger will only hurt you. Learn to forgive the people who have hurt you.

3. **Be respectful of others' boundaries** - After a big argument, some people need their space to process. Give them their space and don't keep going after them to have them talk about the problem. Find ways to calm yourself down such as journaling or going for a walk.

4. **Reflect**- Looking at past situations helps people understand their interpretations of the event that lead them to feel upset. Explore reasons for frustration, and alternative ways of looking at the situation.

Using Rational-Emotive Therapy for Anger

Imagine two customers are waiting in line to buy a cup of coffee, and the cashier is taking a long time to help them. By the time the cashier gets to the two customers, they each have a different reaction: customer 1 feels relieved to finally get her cup of coffee, but customer 2 feels angry and annoyed that the cashier had taken so long. If both customers were dealing with the same exact situation, then why did they feel so differently? The answer is that it is ***the way we perceive a situation, the way we think about an event, that causes our emotional reaction.***

Rational-emotive therapy is a tool, founded by Dr. Albert Ellis, that we can use to help us improve the way we perceive ourselves, others, and life situations. The gist of R.E.T. is that we feel the way we think. When we view something in a negative light, we tend to feel negative emotions. Likewise, if we view things in a positive light, we tend to feel happier. The following section will introduce R.E.T. as a method to help you reduce the occurrence of negative emotions, particularly anger, by helping you identify and ultimately change your belief systems.

The first step is to become more aware of your triggering thoughts. One great way to do this is to write them down. For the next few days, when you feel yourself becoming angry, describe the **situation** that led you to become angry. Next, identify your **beliefs** about the events that took place. Then, try to pinpoint your **feelings** about the situation, as well as what **actions** you took. Finally, if your own thinking triggered you to feel angry, then **dispute** your belief system and choose alternative thoughts and beliefs. Below is an example of what R.E.T. looks like:

1. ***Situation:*** What was the situation that led you to become angry?
2. ***Beliefs & Interpretation:*** How did you interpret the situation?
3. ***Feelings:*** What were your feelings during the situation?
4. ***Actions:*** If you felt anger, what did you do because of your anger?
5. ***Dispute:*** How can you look at the situation differently?

You can alter your feelings and thoughts by changing your beliefs and interpretations of the event. How does this work? Well, beliefs shape the way we think (our thoughts). Our thoughts lead us to feel our feelings. Finally, when we feel a certain way, we are going to act a certain way. The following diagram shows how this idea flows:

Beliefs ⇒ **Thoughts** ⇒ **Feelings** ⇒ **Actions**

For the final step of the R.E.T. process, we question or "dispute" our old beliefs and retrain our minds with updated, positive messages. We want our new beliefs to be more realistic, as they will give us less of a reason to become upset. Use the following questions to help you dispute your outdated beliefs:

- Who said that this is true?
- Why do I believe this?
- Where is my evidence?
- What are some alternative ways of looking at this?

By writing down the situation and working through the steps of the R.E.T. process, we have a visual with which to observe our gradual progress.

The following are examples of how to use R.E.T. for anger:

Situation 1

Situation: While I was walking through the outdoor galleria, I noticed that a number of people were smoking cigarettes.

Beliefs & Interpretation: People should not smoke in a place where others can be affected by the smoke. I have asthma, and now I may get sick. That's so inconsiderate of them!

Feelings: I felt angry and frustrated.

Actions: I started waving my hand in front of my face to get the smoke away from me. I also gave the people dirty looks.

Dispute: As I kept walking, I realized I was in the smoking section of the galleria. They were smoking in the proper section. I could have walked around that area to avoid the smoke.

Situation 2

Situation: I was in a restaurant on a Friday evening with a friend. The waitress sat a family with a crying infant right next to us.

Beliefs & Interpretation: I can't believe a family would take a crying infant to a nice restaurant on a Friday evening. The mother should at least be trying to comfort her infant to quiet him down.

Feelings: Furious and resentful, I felt stressed out that my evening was being ruined.

Action: I gave the family dirty looks to let them know that their crying baby was annoying me.

Dispute: This family certainly has a right to go out together on a Friday night. After all, what are they supposed to do, sit at home just because they have a baby with colic? They should be able to enjoy their evening out, too.

Try it out yourself

Situation 1

Situation:____

Beliefs & Interpretation: ________________________________

____

Feelings:____

Action: ____

Dispute:____

____

Situation 2

Situation:____

Beliefs & Interpretation: ________________________________

____

Feelings:____

Action: ____

Dispute:____

CALL TO ACTION: List several recent situations that were upsetting. For each incident, write your beliefs, how you felt, how you handled it, and how you could have disputed your interpretation of the event.

Debriefing an Argument

In order to improve relationships with others, it is important to hone the skill of debriefing an argument. Having a disagreement is common. Therefore it is encouraged to work through a conflict rather than avoiding the interaction. Debriefing an argument can help with the improvement of communication, and problem solving.

The following demonstrates how to use this worksheet: Debriefing an Argument

1. Describe the situation which led to an argument. *I told my boyfriend last week that I wanted to spend quality time with him for the upcoming weekend. When the weekend arrived I noticed his friends from out of town were at his home as well.*

2. What was your unmet need? *I wanted to feel important and loved.*

3. On a scale of 1 to 10, how hurt were you when your need was unmet? *10!*

4. How did you express your level of hurt? *I gave him the silent treatment. When we were finally alone I told him that he is selfish and careless!*

5. Did any of your feelings possibly relate to your past? *My ex often ignored my feelings; perhaps that may have contributed.*

6. How do you think your partner felt after you expressed yourself? *Guilty, hopefully! But knowing him, he was offended and confused, like always!*

7. Did you get what you needed after you expressed yourself? *No. He was more focused on name calling and blaming than on my feelings.*

8. Did you want to prove that your partner was wrong? *Yes. I did nothing wrong. He was the one who was inconsiderate and careless!*

9. Were there other factors that contributed to the increased level of intensity during the argument such as stress, hunger, and/or lack of sleep? *Maybe. I am financially stressed right now. I guess that's why it was so important for me to have his support over the weekend and to spend quality time just the two of us.*

10. Were there other factors that could have potentially increased the intensity level of the argument for your partner? *No!*

11. What was your partner's perspective on this situation? *He probably assumed we would spend quality time the next day.*

12. Were you able to validate his or her feelings? If so, how? If not, why not? *No, I was too angry and disappointed.*

13. What could you have done differently to get your needs met? *Not judge him or call him names and not be so reactive. I should have expressed my feelings assertively.*

14. What will help you in the future to de-escalate an argument? *Realize I'm emotionally charged and wait to respond rather than react! Also, try to understand the other person's perspective. It takes understanding in order to be understood!*

By answering the following questions, you will improve understanding of situations that are upsetting, and be more likely to see alternative approaches to handling future interactions as they arise.

1. Describe the situation which led to an argument.

2. What was your unmet need?

3. On a scale of 1 to 10, how hurt were you when your need was unmet?

4. How did you express your hurt?

5. Did any of your feelings possibly relate to your past?

6. How do you think your partner felt after you expressed yourself?

7. Did you get what you needed after you expressed yourself?

8. Did you want to prove that your partner was wrong?

9. Were there other factors that contributed to the increased level of intensity during the argument such as stress, hunger, and/or lack of sleep?

10. Were there other factors for your partner that could have potentially increased the intensity level of the argument?

11. What was your partner's perspective in this argument?

12. Were you able to validate his or her feelings? If so, how? If not, why not?

13. What could you have done differently to get your needs met?

14. What will you do in the future to de-escalate an argument?

Arguments

Do you consider yourself someone who argues a lot? Has it ever crossed your mind that your quarrels may actually be bringing on undesirable health conditions? Whether you find yourself arguing with your spouse, children, colleagues, or strangers, learning effective communication strategies will not only help your health, but your relationships as well.

The purpose of this lesson plan is to gain understanding of the impact of arguments on health and relationships, and to pay attention to why we really argue. In your next lesson plan, you will learn the different styles of communication as well as some strategies to more effective communication.

Many times when we envision arguments, we think of yelling and put-downs. Arguments are oral disagreements, verbal oppositions, or discussions involving differing points of view. What's fascinating about arguments is that, in spite of the detrimental effects they may have on our health, they can also be *key* in strengthening our relationships.

Lund and her colleagues studied the impact of arguments on health. They conducted a longitudinal study on 10,000 Danish adults ages 36-52 in 2000. The study was published in May of 2014 in the *Journal of Epidemiology and Community*. Individuals answered questions about **conflicts** with partners, children, other family, friends, and neighbors.

They found that middle-aged adults who frequently argued with their partners were more than twice as likely to die at a relatively young age, compared with people who rarely fought. Frequent confrontations with friends were even more hazardous than conflicts with partners since they were 2.6 times more likely to die prematurely than those who got along with their peers. And can you guess who you *really* should avoid arguing with? **Neighbors**. Neighbors who argue are 3 times more likely to die prematurely than neighbors who get along.

Over the 11 years of the study, 4% of the women and 6% of the men died. The risk showed stronger for men than women. And it was stronger for people who were not working outside the home. What does this say for stay-at-home married men who argue often?

Another study at the New Brigham Young University, led by Rick Miller and his colleagues, also suggests that arguing is bad for your health. This 20-year longitudinal study is considered to be one of the longest on marital quality and health. Marital quality was measured in two ways: (1) in terms of happiness and satisfaction, and; (2) in terms of marital problems, such as arguments.

Miller found that couples who don't argue live longer and those with on-going marital conflicts. Arguing couples were also more likely to report poor health. This implies that marital conflict is a risk factor for poor health. An interesting find through this study is that happy marriages have **a preventative component,** meaning it keeps people in good health throughout the years. Loving couples inspire habits that lead to better health, such as sleeping, and eating better, and drinking less alcohol. In addition, these couples encourage each other to keep doctor's appointments, to take medication as prescribed, and to participate in healthy activities. This type of support reduces stress and, consequently, it helps buffer against a decline in health.

Though the two research studies mentioned focus on the negative effects of arguing on one's health, let's look at what *else* research suggests about the impact of arguments on relationships.

A survey, conducted in India by Shaadi.com, in association with IMRB International, concluded that **couples who argue, stay together**. They looked at some of the essentials to a satisfying marriage and found that communication was very important. 44% of married couples interviewed believe that arguing is what **helps keep the lines of communication open.** But there is clearly a limit: Couples reported that arguing once a week can be the secret to a happy marriage—provided it's not abusive. Only 9% of the respondents reported *daily* disagreements. It's interesting to note that it was the women, more than the men, who were more likely to report their arguments as "frequent."

Fighting and addressing problems constructively makes for a more stress-free relationship than bottling things up. It's **how** couples handle arguments. Arguments are inevitable in a relationship. Understanding **what an argument is *really* about** and **what each party can do** to appease the other might help resolve the issues.

You may think you argue because your partner did something disrespectful. But there's usually an underlying reason to a conflict. If a couple is asked to explain why they are having an argument, each partner may identify a specific event he or she believes to have started the conflict (such as "she forgot to get me the foods I like from the market," or "he criticized my writing"). It's easy to fail at identifying the more important underlying concerns which are triggered by that event, such as having personal needs neglected, or having one's power threatened (Markman, Stanley, & Blumberg, 2001).

Dr. Sue Johnson's theory is that couples argue when they feel disconnected, and their needs go unmet. She sees it as important that you get to the root of conflicts. If you keep peeling the layers of the onion, you will notice the following concerns at the core:

> Do you still love me?
> Do you still admire me?
> Can I still rely on you?
> Are you still attracted to me?
> Am I still important to you?

Dr. Sue Johnson says that **emotional responsiveness** is the key to sustaining a good relationship.

What's important to people during an argument? A study led by Keith Sanford from Baylor University was published in the *Journal of Social and Clinical Psychology* in 2010. 455 married participants were asked to make a list of the resolutions they hoped for in a current or ongoing disagreement with spouses. Members of couples were asked to explain how their partners could change behaviors to resolve a conflict. The researchers used previous studies to identify two main underlying concerns that couples have during conflict:

(a) **perceived neglect**, where one partner feels as though the other is being inattentive or disloyal, and
(b) **perceived threat,** where one partner feels as though the other is being **too critical or demanding**. Here the partner is hostile, critical, blaming, or controlling.

This is important to know since, if the issue of the argument is perceived neglect, then spending more time with your partner may be enough. In contrast, if a person is concerned about a perceived threat, then being more flexible, communicating more effectively, and providing more trust would be essential.

Participants were asked to think about a single, specific episode of conflict in their relationship, and complete the **Couples Underlying Concern Inventory**, where they indicated what words could be used to describe themselves and their partner during a conflict. They were asked to list what their partner could do to resolve the issue. The results reflect that perceived threat bothers couples more, and that it was most important to participants that their partners are **willing to relinquish power** and **stop any "adversarial" behavior.**

When we feel criticized, we experience a perceived threat to our status, at which point we want a partner to disengage and back off. Giving up power may mean to give a partner more independence, to admit fault, show respect, and to compromise.

What's the solution? It sounds like a great place to start is to reduce the frequency of conflicts since it's affecting our health, yet to communicate assertively to develop a longer lasting relationship. In summary, you could focus on the following three points:

1- Understand your wants/needs.
2- Communicate your wants in an assertive manner.
3- Limit frequency of sensitive conversations or confrontations. Choose your battles.

The following lesson plan will cover the different styles of communication and assertive communication skills to be used for sensitive conversations. Have you ever been in a situation where all you did was express yourself, and you thought you were being nice about it, and next thing you know, the receiving person is defensive and attacking you verbally? Many people have, and that's why it's essential to learn assertive communication skills. Most of what we communicate is through body language (67%), then tone (26%), and, least of all, through content (7%).

Understanding Types of Communication

Passive: Passive individuals have difficulty expressing their concerns and feelings and tend to hold them inside. This leads to ineffectively hoping that situations will improve. Since they have difficulty expressing their thoughts, the passive communicator needs for others to read their mind and decipher their distressing thoughts and needs. These individuals are often perceived as shy and reserved.

- The downside of this style is that oftentimes the individual's needs will go unmet, and they become resentful.

Aggressive: Aggressive individuals are able to express their thoughts and feelings; however, they do so by offending those they are communicating with, having little or no regard for the other person's rights or feelings. They tend to lack boundaries and have a need to control their surroundings and relationships.

- Although these people might get what they want in the short term, the consequence of this style is that they get into trouble with others, lose relationships, risk their careers and offend many.

Passive-Aggressive: Most people tend to be passive-aggressive and have difficulty expressing their thoughts and feelings clearly. Consequently, they resort to indirect forms of communication, such as sarcasm, to get their points across, rather than speaking directly about their concerns. Passive-aggressive individuals shy away from conflict or tension, yet they want others to know how they fail. These individuals show their frustration but they don't express themselves verbally and their words don't match their behavior.

- These individuals don't feel heard or understood, despite their attempts at communicating their frustration.
- Although this person is trying to avoid conflict, their behavior creates tension within relationships, often leading to a toxic environment. We're sure you can imagine the confusion and frustration of being on the receiving end of this style.

Assertive: The Assertive approach is considered to be the healthiest and most effective way of communicating. An assertive person expresses thoughts and feelings clearly and directly in a respectful manner. The goal is to understand one another and not to prove the other person wrong. It is a win/win approach. Assertive people are direct, thus reducing the likelihood of misunderstandings. It doesn't mean that others won't get upset by what you are saying, but since it is done in such a respectful and diplomatic manner, your message will be better received. Assertive communication has the highest likelihood of achieving your desired outcome. This style also fosters a sense of trust in others since they know that you are an honest and direct communicator.

Assertive Communication Skills

Remember, the goal of being assertive is to express your thoughts and feelings respectfully. You also want to hear feedback and concerns from your partner.

1. Use "I" statements - *"You" statements tend to get the listener defensive. It is an attacking language. Format to follow: "I feel _______. (I-statements were coined by Thomas Gordon in the 1960's).*

2. State the specific behavior of the other person. *Format to follow: "When you ________." For example: "I feel overwhelmed when you don't have the report in on time."*

3. Acknowledge why you think the person acted or didn't act in a particular way, and let them know what it is you understand. *We like to be heard and understood. This usually reduces the likelihood of getting defensive.*
   For example: "I understand that you're very busy and that it's almost impossible at times...."

4. Say what you want respectfully. *Format to follow: "I would like for you to ________." For example: "I would like for you to get the report in on time."*

5. *Say why it's important (list reasons for what you want). For example: "This is important to me because when your report is not in on time, then my report is also delayed, and I don't want to get into trouble. It's also important so I don't stress and worry as much."*

6. *Know some alternatives. Listing some alternatives can increase the likelihood of a possible change. For example: "If you cannot have the report in on time, please communicate that to me in advance so that I can better prepare myself.*
   I can also potentially help you with the report if I have the time."

***STAY AWAY FROM …* since it creates defensiveness in others**

1. Absolute words such as "always," "never," "everyone," or "no one."
2. "I told you so."
3. "You should or could have…"
4. Giving advice
5. "You" statements
6. Asking "Why" questions… it's accusatory.
7. Bringing other people into the conversation… "______ thinks the same way about you."
8. "I feel that you are ______"

Practice through role-plays. How would you have felt about the message if you were on the receiving end? What could you have done that would have made it more effective?

SCENARIOS for Role Playing to Practice Assertive Communication

Format to communicate assertively:
I feel _______ (feeling word) when you ______ (specific behavior).
I understand __________ (explain your understanding).
I would like ________ (state what you want).
This is important to me because _______ (list reasons for importance).
Some alternatives are _______________ (list some alternatives).

Example of assertive communication:
I feel overwhelmed when you don't have the report in on time. I understand that you're very busy and that it's almost impossible at times. I would like for you to get the report in on time. This is important to me because when your report is not in on time, then my report is also delayed, and I don't want to get into trouble. It's also important so I don't stress and worry as much. If you cannot have the report in on time, please communicate that to me in advance so that I can better prepare myself. I can also potentially help you with the report if I have the time.

Practice assertive communication using the following sample scenarios:

1. You come home to a messy house after work. You have shared with your spouse the importance of keeping the home tidy.

2. A coworker oftentimes leaves their work unfinished; consequently the work becomes yours to complete.

3. It is New Year's Eve and you have 30 minutes remaining for the count down! The taxi you requested arrives 10 minutes later than expected and is charging you double the price!!

4. When you express your feelings or concerns about your relationship with your spouse, they begin to share their thoughts as well and disregard your feelings.

5. Though your friend is aware of your financial struggles, he consistently asks for rides and offers no gas money.

6. Your roommate tells you that they will not be able to pay this month's rent. The rent is due the same day you receive this information. This is the third time they've done this.

7. Your boss discredits your hard work and focuses only on your mistakes.

8. You call your friend to make plans however they give an excuse to reject the offer. Your friend has cancelled plans with you several times in the past month.

Active Listening

Conversations can be tricky, especially between individuals who have ongoing issues with each other or have a stake in the outcome. A conversation with a partner, friend, family member, co-worker, employer, employee, neighbor, or one of your own children can trigger hurt feelings, resentments, and anger which can escalate into an argument that ends up going nowhere and making things worse.

However, by utilizing one or more of the easily learned *active listening techniques* below, one can turn an important conversation from a destructive one into a productive one.

One handy way of remembering the different techniques (tools) is to group them into the four basic phases of a typical "active listening" conversation.

I. Active listening
II. Giving feedback
III. Deepening the conversation
IV. Bringing the conversation to a close

ACTIVE LISTENING

1. ***Encourage the person to talk***: "You seem upset. Would you like to discuss it? Sometimes talking helps."
2. ***Active Listening posture:*** sit back, relax, and make eye contact. This lets the other person know they are free to speak without interruptions or being met with defensiveness.
3. ***Allow Silences***: Even if the speaker pauses, don't interrupt. Let them gather their thoughts or perhaps even get the courage to say something they've been holding back.
4. ***Paraphrase / Restate:*** Occasionally, in order to check out your perceptions and reassure the other person that you've been attending carefully, summarize or paraphrase what they've been saying: "I think you've been telling me ______________. Is that correct?" "Am I getting it right?"

GIVING FEEDBACK

1. ***Receptiveness and Warmth***: Just your physical demeanor may be enough to encourage a person to speak freely. Smile. Nod. Maintain that eye contact.
2. ***Reflecting:*** repeating back the emotional aspects of what is being communicated through incorporating feeling words lets the speaker know you are listening, understanding and showing empathy. For example: "It sounds like you are feeling *taken advantage of* by your friends."

3. ***Supporting, encouraging comments***: Just responding with short, supportive "that's great" or "good for you" phrases can do wonders: "Wow!" "That took courage on your part."
4. ***Acknowledging, Validating, Showing Empathy:*** Acknowledge the person's feelings and issues. This lets the other person know that you understand where they are coming from: "I can see how it's disruptive to your train of thought when I interrupt you."
5. ***Self-disclosing, sharing***: Sometimes, depending on the situation, it's validating to share your own similar experiences and feelings so the speaker realizes they are having normal emotions; they aren't "nuts". The issue is how they can learn to handle these emotions in a more effective way.

DEEPENING THE CONVERSATION

1. ***Naming the emotions:*** Sometimes people aren't clear themselves what they are feeling. After listening to them, you may say something like, "It sounds to me like you are feeling hurt and angry, not 'disappointed'."
2. ***Probing:*** Asking questions is an art and can be done without making the other person feel they are being interrogated, which may put them on the defensive. "Tell me more," "What happened then?", "What was that like?", "How did that feel on a scale of 1-10?" or, "Was that difficult?" You can keep things short with: "How? When? Where?"
3. ***Interpreting:*** Offering some suggestions about the other person's feelings, needs, and concerns, is intended to give them insight and make future experiences with these feelings easier.
4. ***Consequences:*** At a deeper phase of the conversation, the person may be emotionally ready to start taking a look at the impact of their communication style on others, and face the price they've been paying for poor communication. Ask questions related to these consequences: "Have you thought about how yelling at people may shut them down or instill fear?" "At work, how did you deal with that situation and how did it turn out? Did it help?"
5. ***"I" Messages:*** "When you ____ I feel ____," or, "I need to tell you _____," or, "How I look at it is______________" are important aspects of active listening that show that each person has a point of view that's not a blaming, "right/wrong" stance, but rather a realistic "you/me" message.

BRINGING THE CONVERSATION TO A CLOSE

1. ***Redirecting:*** If the person speaking seems to be getting worked up and more upset, or angry, then it may be a sign that it's time to shift the topic or even stop the discussion for now, and suggest that the talk be continued at a later date.
2. ***Summing Up:*** One way to draw the conversation to a close is to sum up what the two of you have been discussing, re-state the problem, and decide upon a goal, such as finding a better way to deal with a problem.

3. ***Action Plan:*** Perhaps the conversation can end with an agreed-upon task or something to practice (waiting to cool down before responding to an upsetting situation, for example). Once one "good communication" has taken place, it usually paves the way for more to follow.

HARMFUL LISTENING HABITS

There are many circumstances where people disrupt a good communication flow. Let's look at some harmful listening habits.

1. Judging what the speaker is saying.
2. Assuming you know what the speaker will say.
3. Not keeping your own emotions in check about what's being discussed.
4. Interrupting the speaker.
5. Changing the subject without acknowledging.
6. Not acknowledging the person when they speak.
7. Looking distracted while a person is talking to you. *Put your phone away.*
8. Trying to formulate your response instead of being present with the speaker.
9. Offering solutions/ fixing the problem.

Here are a few example statements you could work with for now. Try to use as many of the active listening techniques as possible to become more comfortable with utilizing the tools.

1. Your co-worker tells you the following:

   I really think there's favoritism in our company. I never get my requests approved yet everyone else always seems to get what they want. This happens to me all the time.

2. Your mother tells you the following:

   I wish you called more often because I miss you. I've been lonely, and of course I worry about you. Both you and your brother seem to have very busy lives. I didn't realize how lonely I was going to end up feeling.

3. Your significant other tells you the following:

   I really need some help around the house. I've asked several times, but I really wish you would just do them without my needing to ask. I have so much on my plate, so it would really help if you did some of the work around here.

CALL TO ACTION: Try practicing active listening skills with those close to you.

What if People are Not Responding to Me?

Wouldn't life be wonderful if people responded the way we'd like them to? If you've been practicing the skills you've learned from your anger management class and you're still not getting the results you'd like, continue working on yourself.

Sometimes it's hard to figure out just why a person is not responding. The reasons may not be obvious, not even to them. But don't give up. Read what's below to see if some of it applies to you and might be contributing to why the other person isn't responding positively to your attempts to engage in a sensitive conversation:

1. **"It's Useless."** Sometimes people don't engage in sensitive conversations with you because they don't think it's going to do any good; it won't change anything. Conceivably they've had interactions with you in the past where they ended up feeling like the loser. And they may not have had any contrasting experiences during which they felt their wants and needs were being served. A sensitive conversation takes effort, and it takes emotional investment. So who would want to put all that effort into having a sensitive conversation if it doesn't do them any good? You'll have to find ways of showing your openness to the other person's opinions and needs, starting with smaller conversations first and then, over time, their trust will be restored enough to risk engaging in *sensitive* conversations.

2. **The need for feeling safe.** The other person may not be feeling "safe" in a conversation with you. They may be feeling disrespected or unsure that you really have their best interests at heart.

3. **Situational Safety vs. Relational Safety:** *Situational safety* means that it's just in *this particular conversation* that they don't feel safe with you (in which case applying some of the communication skills you've learned may help). On the other hand, *relational safety* means that the other person hasn't felt safe or respected in conversations with you over a sustained period of time (in which case the problem won't yield to the simple application of a few learned "skills"). You'll first need to acknowledge that you may have contributed to the other person's feeling of "lack of safety," and you must make a commitment to changing your behavior. And then *do* it. Respectful communication and safety won't be fully restored until you've changed your actions. Then, over time, you'll find that people begin to feel safer with you and they begin to engage more trustingly in *sensitive conversations*.

4. **It's Not Mutual:** Another possibility is that the other person may feel comfortable having discussions with you about certain topics, but when it comes to a *specific* sensitive conversation, it holds no benefit for them. In order to have *this* conversation, you have to have a *mutual purpose, problem or goal.* The sensitive conversation you then need to hold is one in which you help them understand the significant benefits of

engaging in this particular dialogue with you in order to resolve it one way or the other and not leave it hanging.

5. **Too High-Maintenance:** Some people want to have a "sensitive conversation" over every little issue. There's always some problem they feel must be discussed. This can be draining to others and they'll start seeing you as too "high-maintenance" and want to avoid you. The idea of yet another drawn-out discussion is too exhausting to contemplate. Learn to let some issues slide; be more understanding and accepting. Begin to rebuild your relational safety by creating nourishing and enjoyable interactions. Stop creating a heavy environment. You *want* others to find interactions with you fun and pleasurable, so change their experience of you by changing the type of interactions you have together. A bit more tolerance and patience on your part may result in their wanting to talk to you without fear of "high-maintenance fatigue".

Summary: Hopefully, these observations and suggestions will help you reflect on what's going on in your various relationships as far as sensitive conversations are concerned, and give you some ideas to help you create the results that are important to you. Though these *skills don't guarantee that people will respond, they do increase the likelihood that you'll both be heard.* At the very least, you can tell yourself that you tried.

Joseph Grenny is the author of three bestselling books: Influencer, Crucial Conversations, and *Crucial Confrontations.*

De-Escalating an Argument

People in relationships tend to develop their own style of communicating with each other and handling conflicts. Sometimes they get stuck in a pattern of response and don't have the flexibility to try other techniques that might work better. For example, one person may be more tolerant and stoic, while the other may be more passionate or emotional. Usually, it's the more passionate and emotional one who ends up carrying the burden of worry or anger in the relationship, and they may feel shut out by the one who is stoic and less reactive. The more they push at each other to get the kind of response they want, the more things escalate in a negative way. This creates a high level of anxiety in the relationship because neither knows what the other person is thinking or feeling or what they want.

Given that individuals may have developed styles that are more like oil and water together, let's look at some strategies that might help them get unstuck from their unworkable styles and discover ways to express concern, sympathy and empathy for each other. This hopefully results in a smoother resolution to a problem – not just another argument.

Select the strategies you feel might be helpful to you with your own relationship situation:

1. When a discussion gets overwhelming, and you feel you need your space, be sure to communicate that to the other person. Explain that you need space to process your own emotions, but that you'll return to the discussion within a specified time frame.

2. When someone is talking and giving you more information than you can take in at one time, ask for a time-out. Validate that what they are saying is important, and that you want to give it your full attention, but that it would be more beneficial to take a little break so that you can reflect on what's been discussed. Don't keep trying to listen when you can't give the other person your full attention since this will just spark more conflict.

3. Refrain from "fixing" or "problem solving." Rather, incorporate active listening skills. Be a sounding board for the other person; encourage them to talk. It will help them through their difficulties. It's usually the less emotional one who tries to "fix" the problem. They think they are being helpful, but in actuality it's just making things worse. The message it gives the other person is, "You can't handle it when I'm upset, and you want me to be all better."

4. When someone is upset, you don't have to take the blame for their problems. It's easy to feel guilty or responsible when they communicate in ways that make it sound as if you are at fault. Do your best to listen, understand, and validate.

5. Even if they ask for it, still don't offer your opinions, advice, or any solutions because, again, it implies that you know more about what's good for them than they do. Instead, ask them what options they've considered, and ask what they think are some of the pros and cons of each. This will reinforce that what they think is valuable and important, and that they have what it takes to come up with great decisions.

6. Misunderstandings are behind many heated arguments. It's so easy for a discussion to get derailed in this way. Therefore, prior to responding, check with your partner to make sure you're hearing them correctly. For example, "I hear you saying that you're disappointed in me because I don't help around the home as much as you would like, is that correct?" Once you have the

green light, then respond and offer your viewpoint.

7. You will have disagreements in views and opinions. When this happens, ask how your partner reached their conclusions before you respond. Acknowledge what you like about their thinking. You can understand why they've reached their conclusions without necessarily needing to agree with their viewpoints.

8. Refrain from providing false hope, or making pacifying statements. For example, don't say, "It's going to be alright." You don't know that, and it's not necessarily helpful to hear. It's also okay if the other individual cries. Try to offer support by listening and being there with them.

9. Validate their feelings. Avoid cliche phrases such as, "Don't worry about it," or "Don't feel that way." These invalidating statements may actually make a person feel unheard. Instead, try validating by saying, "I can see how it impacts your schedule when I don't keep up with my share of the household chores."

10. Label the feelings of anger and disappointment that you can see the other individual is feeling towards you: "You are dissatisfied with me because____." This will soften their attack because they will feel heard and understood.

Conflict Resolution

When you are the target of someone else's anger or disappointment, it may be hard for you to keep your cool and utilize the tools you've learned to combat this kind of situation, especially if the other person is bombarding you with yelling and threats. You may even find yourself falling back on old coping styles, such as yelling back or going on the defensive. Such responses usually come from still not feeling solid inside about your beliefs and standards. It takes a while, but once you become more self-aware, you'll be able to handle these scenes more efficiently.

In some cases, both parties may become emotional and go on the defensive at the same time, attacking each other, and trying to get their points across while the other is not listening. This causes the situation to escalate, as neither one can calm down long enough to try to break this cycle of back and forth yelling.

Whatever the situation, practicing one or more of the nine strategies below may help:

1. Accept that you will make mistakes. This allows you to take a sincere look at yourself by understanding your flaws objectively rather than blaming yourself.

2. When there is any truth to the criticism being leveled at you by the other person, agree with it, and state how that possibly contributed to the current problem. This will help with deescalating an argument because the person will feel heard and understood.

3. State specifically what you are apologizing for, rather than just issuing a vague, "I'm sorry." Express your remorse with sincerity, and sympathize with the other person's concerns. Acknowledge how what you did impacted them.

4. If there are specific changes you can make, share this with the other individual. However, be sure to follow through with what you've promised. If the change is not realistic, then don't make false promises.

5. Once you've been confronted by someone, explore whether or not their complaint is reasonable. Run the situation by some friends who seem to have good relationships and ask for their input. If you realize that there are indeed things about yourself that you could change which might improve things, then take some steps towards that end. However, make sure the actions fit who you are. If you take on more "change" than you're ready for, you may end up feeling resentful.

6. It is okay if you decide to not make any changes. What is important is that you have heard the other individual, and you've shown compassion and empathy for their complaints about you. Be sincere when you inform them that while you can understand their view of you, you are not planning on making any changes at this time.

7. If an individual in your life is very giving, be sure to give back as well. Offer acts of kindness, your time, or what feels appropriate. Ask if you can help or contribute in any way.

8. If the other person tends to be passive and not speak up about their wants and needs, help them along by asking for their preferences. It's easy for decisions to keep going your way, but understand that the other person may become silently resentful. So remember to take turns on suggestions or making decisions.

9. If old issues in a relationship keep coming up, then something has been left unresolved. Practice your newly learned listening skills and offer support and your attention. You could also ask what triggered the old issue at this time. For many, it's frustrating to have to discuss old issues over and over again. However, people do need to work through the underlying problems in order for the relationships to progress.

When it Gets Pretty Bad and You've Tried Other Strategies

In many relationships, one person learns that they have to yell in order to be heard. If the other one is silent, the first one yells even more. Unfortunately, this creates problems.

When you think an argument is getting out of hand, it's easy to feel powerless and helpless. Remind yourself that the other person is yelling because they, too, feel powerless and are raising their voice as a way to get heard.

Below are a few strategies that may help you through this type of situation:

1. If you're unable to engage in a calm discussion, leave the room and do something to soothe yourself. Assure the other person you will discuss this later.

2. If you do have the strength to withstand the storm, focus on the other person. Do not interrupt. While you're looking at them, keep asking yourself, "What is really hurting him or her?" This is especially difficult to do while you are under attack.

3. Point out what's going on, and ask for what you want. If you are feeling scared, let the other person know that their yelling is scaring you. You can even state, "I don't like that we are arguing. I would really like a hug and to hear that we will be okay."

4. When you see an opening, show that you understand the other person's point of view.

5. When the participants in an argument are very heated, it's not a good time to try reasoning or disagreeing with them. Individuals are unable to hear when they are fuming. Stop. Wait. Resolve it later.

Emotional Intelligence and Empathy

Identifying your emotions and understanding others' behaviors

What is Emotional Intelligence (EI)?

EI is a type of intelligence where the focus is on social and emotional competency. It includes the ability to understand how you impact others and how others impact you, and to use that information to help develop better relations with the people in your life. In addition, emotional intelligence involves understanding your thoughts and emotions, and using that information to manage your behavior and accompanying actions.

Daniel Goleman, a well-known psychologist, popularized the notion of emotional intelligence. According to his works, the qualities below reflect some of the key components of emotional intelligence that can help people interact more effectively with others in various situations. The components include:

1. **Self-awareness** --- the capacity to understand yourself, including your thoughts and feelings
2. **Self-regulation** --- the ability to manage your impulses and behaviors, and adapt to uncomfortable situations involving yourself or others
3. **Social skill** --- the awareness of how you impact your surroundings and how others impact you, and the ability to use this knowledge to improve your relations
4. **Empathy** --- the ability to consider and understand others' perspectives and feelings

What Is Empathy?

Empathy, one of the constructs of emotional intelligence, is a particularly effective skill you can use to help alleviate feelings of anger. The ability to see life through someone else's perspective, otherwise known as *"putting yourself in someone else's shoes,"* is the essence of empathy. It is the intellectual and emotional understanding of another person's feelings, thoughts, and/or experiences. By accessing your own emotions, ones that are similar to what the other person is feeling in the moment, you have the opportunity to understand and better relate to him or her.

Why Do We Use Empathy?

We use empathy to convey our understanding of loved ones, as well as to better relate to their experiences. By doing so, a connection is created and intimacy begins to build. When people sense that you are attempting to understand their situation, trust, openness, and emotional safety build. In addition, the more you use empathy, the more you will notice other people's appreciation of your understanding. Finally, a higher degree of empathy results in healthier, more meaningful, and respectful relationships.

How Do We Use Empathy?

Learning to use empathy is a process that takes time, but it is not difficult to do. When you are in a situation with a loved one who is upset, see if you can identify what the other person is feeling. If you're unsure, try referring to your own memories of related scenarios, and see what feeling comes up for you---most likely, the emotion you felt may be similar to what the other person is currently feeling. Next, try to communicate this information to them with gentleness and compassion. You can say something like, "Based on what happened, you're probably feeling sad/hurt/afraid right now, and I want you to know that I care about you." By doing so, you validate someone else's feelings, which will increase the likelihood of that person feeling heard and understood.

Exercise: Accessing Emotional Intelligence

Based on the information mentioned above, the following exercise can help you identify your reactions to people's behaviors, understand how they correlate to your understanding of their behaviors, and use the information when you communicate your concerns and needs.

Read and complete the following sentences with: (1) your interpretation or thought of the situation and (2) your feelings about how you perceived the event. For example:

"When you didn't talk to me about what was bothering you, I thought that to mean that you don't trust me, and about that I felt shut out and hurt."

1. *"When you corrected me in front of the boss and the rest of the team, I thought*

   ____

   ______________, *and about that I felt* ______________________________"

2. *"When I came home from work and you didn't greet me, I thought*

   ____

   ____________________ *and about that I felt* ______________________________"

3. *"When you teased me in front of my parents, I thought*

   ____ *and about that I felt* ____________________"

4. *"When you were out with your friends and came home much later than you promised, I thought ____ and about that I felt ______________________________ "*

5. *"When I heard that you shared my confidential information with others without my knowledge, I thought ____ and about that I felt ______________________________ "*

6. *"When you used your bonus to buy a new television instead of paying our debt, I thought ____ and about that I felt ______________________________ "*

7. *"When you check your phone while I speak to you, I thought ____________________ ____ and about that I felt ____________________ "*

8. *"When you look at other men/women while I'm with you, I thought ________________ ______________________________ and about that I felt ____________________ "*

Notice how in each example, the sentence says *"I felt"* before a feeling is expressed, as opposed to *"you made me feel."* The reasoning behind this wording is that no one can "*make*" you feel a certain way. Each person has his/her own individual actions, and the responsibility falls upon you to interpret and perceive other peoples' actions however you choose. In other words, your *perception* of others' actions or words is what triggers you to feel a certain way.

Now, go back and check to see if you responded to any of the statements with anger-related words. Keep in mind, there are almost 130 words that are in the anger family! If you did, review the list and try to identify some other emotions that may have been underlying your anger. It is very easy to resort to "I am angry," so the challenge is to identify and express the underlying, primary emotion (i.e. sad/hurt/afraid/rejected). You might not feel the primary emotion as strongly as you would feel anger, but write it down anyway.

Accessing Empathy

How do you currently identify others' emotions? Is it through body language? If so, what do you look for? Part of Emotional Intelligence is to understand what happens to us during an incident. When trying to express your feelings, take a moment to step out of your shoes and see the other person's perspective.

In each situation presented in the previous exercise or provided by your facilitator, identify ways of understanding the reasons why someone may have acted in a particular way. Keep in mind that this involves putting yourself in his/her shoes in a neutral way without being suspicious or distrustful of his/her actions.

Below are the same situations as listed above. Review them again; this time, however, describe reasons for the person's behavior by putting yourself in his/her shoes. For example, for the following situation:

You didn't talk to me about what was bothering you. Maybe it's because I reacted angrily in the past, and it worried you that I may have responded similarly.

1. *Situation: You corrected me in front of the boss and the rest of the team.*

   ____

2. *Situation: I came home from work and you didn't greet me.*

   ____

3. *Situation: You teased me in front of my parents.*

   ____

4. *Situation: You were out with your friends and came home much later than you promised.*

   ____

5. *Situation: I heard that you shared my confidential information with others without my knowledge.*

   ____

6. *Situation: You used your bonus to buy a new television instead of paying our debt.*

   ____

7. *Situation: You check your phone while I speak to you.*

   ____

8. *Situation: You look at other men/women while I'm with you.*

   ____

The more empathy one has, the less angry or upset one will feel. Empathy and anger are inversely proportional.

Reacting versus Responding

We live in a society where immediate gratification is part of our daily lives. When difficult situations arise, such as triggering emails or upsetting voicemails, people sometimes want to respond right away because the pain is so intolerable. It is challenging for many to take the time to reply and consider their responses to such events. When people react right away instead of choosing healthy responses, they can dig themselves into quite a mess.

Afterward, they may wonder how the situation escalated so quickly. They may ask themselves questions such as, "What happened?" or "How did he end up leaving?" Unfortunately, they will have little success in finding a satisfying answer. The way through is to understand the differences between reacting and responding.

Reacting

When we react, we take action while feeling emotionally charged. It is not a good time to reply to a triggering email or upsetting voicemail when we are in this emotional state. Let's say, for example, that you received a triggering email. Your initial reaction may be to respond in an attacking manner. An alternative is to hold off from replying to the email until the following day. One option is to write an email draft without sending it then reread it the following day. Most likely, you will notice that the draft has a tone that sounds harsh, defensive, and/or attacking. Now, consider writing a new email when you are not feeling as emotionally charged, and you will probably see a difference between the initial draft and the final one. This difference could potentially save a friendship.

Responding

Responding, as opposed to reacting, requires you to cool off and work through the issue before taking action. By doing so, you can explore and understand what is really bothering you about the situation, and get clear on any wants and needs you may feel are necessary to share with the other person. During the waiting process, one option is to journal through your own destructive thinking and hurtful feelings. Another option is to call a trusted person with whom to share your feelings and brainstorm, about how to productively handle the situation. These practices will increase the likelihood of saving important relationships and friendships.

How to Choose Differently

<u>Example 1:</u> My supervisor criticizes me at work, and I:

a. feel angry and resentful. I go into a state of withdrawal and my work suffers. (reacting)

b. recognize that my work does not have to be perfect, and I realize that my supervisor was probably only trying to help me. I continue on with my work. (responding)

<u>Example 2</u>: I receive a disturbing email, and I:

a. write an entire page in return, defending myself and venting my frustrations, potentially losing the friendship. (reacting)

b. journal through my anger, fear, and concern, and work towards understanding my feelings, as well as the other person's point of view. Then I write an email expressing my thoughts and feelings respectfully, and I negotiate by requesting my needs and wants. (responding)

Sample Situations for Practice

1. Situation: My supervisor criticized my work.

   Reacting: ____________________

   Responding: ____________________

2. **Situation:** A worker from a previous shift left work for me which should have been completed during his shift.

   Reacting: ____________________

   Responding: ____________________

3. **Situation:** My mom keeps me on the phone long after I want to talk.

   Reacting: ____________________

   Responding: ____________________

Your Situations

List any recent situations where you reacted:

1- Situation: ____________________
   a. How did you react?
   ____
   ____
   b. How could you have responded?
   ____
   ____

2- Situation: ____________________
   a. How did you react?
   ____
   ____
   b. How could you have responded?
   ____
   ____

The Illusion of Control

Trying to control other people, as well as our own emotional reactions to them, can be very hard to do. Often we're not successful at it. Although we know this intellectually, we still spend a lot of energy trying to control what can't be controlled.

Trying to Control Others

When you attempt to control someone else, you are assuming that they *should* behave, act, think, feel, and believe as you do. The problem is, other people don't like feeling controlled, and neither do you. Not only does being controlling send a message to another person that you don't accept them for who they are, but you are also telling them that you don't trust their judgment. Though you may be able to influence someone to think differently for a time, in the long run you cannot really control or change them. It's usually a useless pursuit.

During the process of trying to control someone else, you usually end up feeling more frustrated and conflicted because you sense that you are basically spinning your wheels. You're doing something that's bound to have an unsatisfying outcome. A much better goal would be to try to become more understanding and accepting of others.

Controlling Statements

The list below includes sample situations of trying to control others. Place a checkmark next to the ones that describe you:

1. I raise my voice and use anger to be heard.
2. When others offer opinions that don't align with mine, I discount what they say and make them wrong.
3. When someone is sharing their opinion, I may appear to be listening, but I'm really just rehearsing my response so I can convince them to see something my way.
4. I frequently offer advice and solutions even though my opinion hasn't been sought.
5. I sometimes lecture people when they don't see things my way.
6. I impose my values onto others even when they are uninterested in hearing about them.
7. I often use absolute statements such as "You should," "You ought to," or "You never."
8. When trying to have a discussion with someone, I end up interrupting them and telling them what to think so they don't have a chance to get their message across.
9. When I'm upset with someone, I procrastinate and don't put much effort into a situation, almost as a way of getting back at them.

10. When I want to get my way, I revert to rigid statements and noncompliance.
11. I use "the silent treatment" as a means of controlling a situation.
12. Sometimes I agree with others just to pacify them.

Trying to Control Your Own Emotional Reactions

Avoiding painful emotions by running away from them doesn't work. When unpleasant feelings surface and you stuff them or distract yourself from them, guess what you get? -- *more* unpleasant feelings! When people seek to banish their emotional pain, they just end up doubling their suffering.

As you go through the list below, check which ones apply to you:

1. As soon as I feel an unwanted emotion, I do what I can to get rid of it.
2. I do not share my problems with others.
3. I do not express my wants and needs with others.
4. I avoid confrontations and controversial topics.
5. I prefer to get rid of upsetting thoughts rather than to explore and understand them.
6. When there are problems, I withdraw rather than work towards resolving them.
7. I often doubt myself and my own decisions.
8. I pretend that everything is okay and I hide any feelings of resentment.
9. I don't express my feelings since I don't believe that telling people about my emotional pain will help me.
10. I spend a lot of energy trying to appear as if I have it all together.
11. I often stuff my feelings or use distractions such as drugs or partying to feel better.
12. I make the needs of others my priority, and neglect my own needs.

In summary, what works best is to accept and deal with emotions as they come up in order to move on through them. Practicing mindfulness techniques, journal writing to explore your thoughts, and talking to people you trust about your concerns are some examples of healthy ways of dealing with your emotional pain.

What's Within Your Influence?

Think of a current or typical situation that is stressful for you.

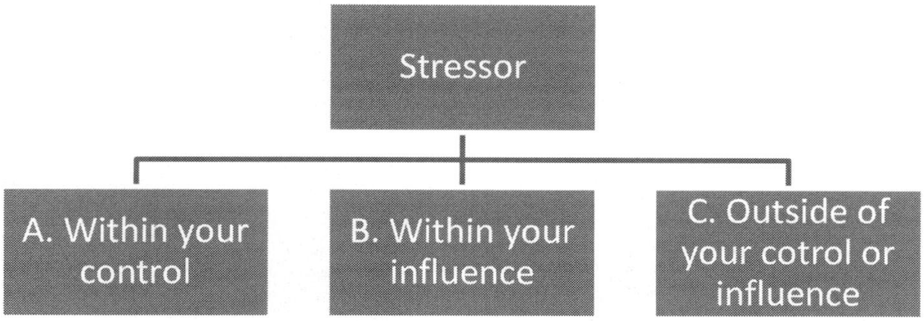

Category C: area outside your control
Putting energy into "C" can lead to feelings of frustration, powerlessness and resentment.

Examples of category C include: weather, traffic, capped salaries, aging and laws.

Category B: area within your influence
Putting energy into "B" leads to clarity and knowledge.

Examples of category B include: relationships, health, and career advancement.

Category A: area within your control
Putting energy into "A" leads to the sense of efficacy, self-esteem, differentiation, and emotional intelligence.

Examples of category A include: decision making, beliefs (religious beliefs, political views), how we dress, where we live, who we marry, what we do for work, and how we spend money.

Exercise: List your stressors in the following table. A stressor is any change that may create stress, including something that is positive such as planning a wedding.

1.	9.
2.	10.
3.	11.
4.	12.
5.	13.
6.	14.
7.	15.
8.	16.

Next: Place the stressor into the appropriate categories below.

Category C: area outside your control

Category B: area within your influence

Category A: area within your control

Where do you spend most of your energy? Do you often think of changing the items that are outside of your control? Your goal: Spend your energy in the areas that are within your control and influence rather than in the area outside your control.

Judging and Labeling

Being judgmental (looking down on others in a superior and condescending way) can be natural, but it is not always helpful.

Being judgmental has its advantages and disadvantages.

Advantages of being judgmental - It helps to determine the types of people we allow into our lives and the amount of trust we give to them. Being judgmental can be a signal that we are not comfortable with a particular type of person. If there is danger, this can be helpful.
The world is full of judges. We are judged by our credit rating, our employment history, our education and our marital status.

Disadvantages of being judgmental - Not only does it increase negative thoughts interpersonally, but when others sense a judgmental attitude, they may become intimidated and refrain from disclosing information for fear of being judged. Moreover so, it shows your emotional intelligence to be very low. For example, when you call someone "stupid," you lower your own value and social status (notice how confident individuals do not resort to putting others down). In most scenarios, being judgmental can be very harmful, since it limits positive opportunities for ourselves.

Where does it begin?
How does being judgmental start? We tend to hear many judgmental comments during childhood and adolescence. In high school, bullies instill fear in other children by putting down the underdog verbally and physically. During adulthood, those who continue those behaviors may appear fixated. These are beliefs that are created early on and ones we carry with us throughout our lives by we placing ourselves in situations that reinforce those same unhealthy beliefs.

It is important though, to notice the feelings that come up when we pass judgment on someone. We may notice another person act in a particular way that doesn't quite correspond with our values, and in turn, become upset due to that dissonance. Take, for example, the following situation: Mary and Mike agreed to meet at 7 PM, but Mary was 30 minutes late. Mike was quick to judge Mary as inconsiderate and disrespectful. How do you think Mike feels when he sees Mary as disrespectful? What are some other ways Mike could approach the situation that would be more productive and less "negatively oriented"?

Taking the time once a day to build a bridge with one person can make a big difference.

The following exercise will help you <u>describe</u> what you think is aversive about someone, as opposed to categorizing or labeling him/her. Remember, when we label people, it allows us to depersonalize them. Let the focus be on you without having to compete for the power. The attempt to stay in power reflects the fear of not having any.

Exercise: Review the following words slowly, and identify your feeling(s) as you review each word. Write your feeling(s) next to each word. Example: "Psycho" - Anger

1. Stupid - ____________________
2. Gold-Digger - ____________________
3. Pig - ____________________
4. Fat - ____________________
5. Crazy - ____________________
6. Promiscuous - ____________________
7. Lazy -____________________

Replace the following words using feelings of empathy, with words that are non-offensive: Example: "Psycho"- I'm upset because he called me three times in one day.

1. Stupid - ____________________
2. Gold-Digger - ____________________
3. Pig - ____________________
4. Fat - ____________________
5. Crazy - ____________________
6. Promiscuous - ____________________
7. Lazy -____________________

What Underlies Labeling / Categorizing / Generalizing

In this next exercise, try to determine the underlying reason a person would label someone or call someone names. For example: "Psycho"- By calling that person psycho, I no longer have to deal with the emotions that surface within me. The problem is theirs, not mine.

1. Stupid - ____
____
2. Gold-Digger - ____
____
3. Pig -____
____
4. Fat - ____
____
5. Crazy - ____
____
6. Promiscuous - ____
____
7. Lazy -____
____

Notice the difference between labeling someone versus properly observing and explaining what you see. This will help you become less frustrated and more at peace in the future.

In the next few days, try to observe when and how often you are having judgmental thoughts.

*Remind yourself to observe and, when ready, try to have empathy and understanding towards the other person by placing yourself in his/her shoes.

*Remember to have empathy and understanding towards yourself, too; you are doing the very best you know how to do, given the tools you have at the time.

*Try to imagine more positive circumstances that might have led the person to act in that way.

*The next step is to accept the person without trying to change them. The world is what it is, and you must learn to adapt to it. Without the willingness to adapt, your future is likely to be very frustrating.

The Misperception of "Disrespect"

In anger management programs, the words "respect" and "disrespect" are often heard. Mostly clients use the word "disrespectful" to refer to others' behavior. Let's explore what it actually means to be disrespected.

To begin, it is important to define the term "respect." According to Merriam-Webster, "respect" means a high or special regard. According to www.Dictionary.com, "respect" is defined as the following: deference to a right, privilege; proper acceptance or courtesy; and acknowledgment. Thus, when a person states that they are feeling disrespected, they are probably feeling disregarded or unacknowledged.

Even though the dictionary has a specific definition for "respect," the word can mean something very different from one person to another. Since people have different life experiences and beliefs, their versions of "respectful" will vary. Consequently, when person A has certain beliefs about how person B should behave in certain situations, and person B acts differently from what person A expects, person A will then think person B is being disrespectful.

Let's take a look at Tony's situation - one in which he feels disrespected.

Situation: My girlfriend does not spend time with me when we are at events together. She interacts with her friends most of the time, but not with me.

Belief: A partner should be by the side of a significant other at social events; otherwise, it is not a good relationship. My friends will question my girlfriend's loyalty to me, and I will look like a fool.

Exploring and understanding what underlies my belief and the feeling of disrespect:
The purpose of this belief is to help me feel emotionally safe with my partner.
I feel disrespected when my girlfriend leaves my side for a little while. I start to think, "She prefers being with her friends over being with me," and I begin to
feel disregarded and hurt. My discomfort with feeling hurt becomes overwhelming and my defense mechanism takes over. Instead of connecting with my emotional pain and taking responsibility for it, I accuse my partner of "disrespecting" me.

Notice how Tony attributes the responsibility of his pain to his girlfriend? He is holding his girlfriend responsible for his own emotional pain, and expects her to change her behavior (which he labels as disrespectful), rather than changing his own belief and thought around the situation (owning his emotion and belief). By stating, "She disrespected me," Tony is essentially victimizing himself. He is giving his partner power over his feelings.

Taking Responsibility for our Own Pain
The truth is, when we put the responsibility of our own emotional pain onto others, we are expecting *them* to change. By doing so, we give away our power. Why on earth do we do that? *It is easier to demand or ask those around us to change, rather than to do the work ourselves.* By changing our thoughts and perceptions, though, we have the power to change our emotions.

Practice

At this point, you may be thinking, "Well, at what point am I *not* supposed to be okay with what my partner is doing?" That's a great question and it is frequently asked. You need to have your own personal set of boundaries that feels comfortable to you. At the same time, to help you gauge your perceptions of others' behavior, you can ask yourself, "Is this belief helping me or hurting me?" Or, if you have friends that seem to have healthy relationships, ask them how they might perceive the same situation.

The good news is that beliefs that result in feeling disrespected are learned, which means that *they can also be unlearned.* When you replace the unhealthy belief with one that is healthier, you will rarely feel disrespected, because your misperception of the situation will change. Your improved insight of the underlying thoughts and feelings of disrespect will help with building healthier relationships.

Now, review the following set of sample questions in order to better understand what underlies the feeling of disrespect.

1. **Describe a situation when you felt disrespected**: *I was at a party and my girlfriend was disrespecting me by spending most of the time with her friends and not me.*

2. **What is the belief that supports your feeling of disrespect in the situation?** *Partners should be together at social events; otherwise, it's not a good relationship. Friends will question the loyalty of my girlfriend to me, and I'll look like a fool.*

3. **What are some thoughts around this situation?**
   a. *She knows it upsets me when she's not by my side at events, and she still does it.*
   b. *She prefers being with her friends rather than with me.*
   c. *I deserve to be with someone who values and respects me.*

4. **Who do you hold responsible for your feeling?** *Her.*

5. **What is the underlying feeling? Hint: don't list feelings in the angry family.** *I'm feeling insecure that others are seeing our relationship as if she wears the pants. I'm also feeling disregarded that she doesn't care about me.*

6. **How would your friends and/or family (ones who are healthy) perceive the situation?** *They are better able to handle it than I. I don't usually hear them complain of situations that are upsetting to me, but then again, they may not be as verbal as I am. They may think that it's okay for their partner to be socializing with others at an event. The purpose of get-togethers is to mingle with friends and family.*

7. **If you gave the benefit of the doubt and were more trusting, what are some other ways you could perceive this situation?** *She says she loves me and cares about me. She's been with me for many years. She rarely gets to see her friend, and does spend time with me when we're at home. And it's not like she completely ignores me at events.*

Describe a situation in which you felt disrespected:

____

____

What is the belief that supported your feeling of disrespect in the situation?

____

____

What are some thoughts around this situation?

____

____

Who do you hold responsible for your feeling?

____

What is the underlying feeling? (hint: don't list feelings in the angry family).

____

How would your friends and/or family (ones who are healthy) perceive the situation?

____

____

If you gave the benefit of the doubt and were more trusting, what are some other ways you could perceive this situation? ______________________________

____

The next time you feel disrespected, try out this worksheet format and question your underlying thoughts and beliefs. Over time, you may notice a change in your own perception of "disrespect".

Jealousy!

Most people are not comfortable admitting that they feel jealous. Perhaps it's because they are afraid others will judge them as insecure or suffering from not feeling "good enough" or attractive enough. Often, jealousy is an attempt to control someone.

Wikipedia defines **JEALOUSY** as a secondary emotion that typically triggers negative thoughts and feelings of insecurity, fear, and anxiety over an anticipated loss of something (a relationship) or someone (the person they are in the relationship with). Jealousy involves a rainbow of emotions – anger, sadness, resentment, and disgust, all of which are different from *envy* which means wanting what someone else *has* rather than fearing the loss of something you have.

As with most emotions, jealousy exists for a reason. It serves a purpose. It can help a person learn a lesson in humility. It can serve as a motivator for taking action. Or it can be an intuitive indicator that something is wrong with a relationship and that a person needs to take steps to protect themselves emotionally. For example, if you suspect that your partner is cheating on you, the feeling may motivate you to ask some vital questions and open up a sensitive conversation in order to learn the truth.

How do you express yourself when you feel jealous? How do you act?

When jealousy is mishandled, it can create problems within a relationship. Many times the jealous person becomes more and more controlling. For example, a jealous person might ask their partner to cancel the partner's plans. But just because a person feels jealous, it does not mean that the other person is required to make changes in their behavior. It's actually best that the partner continues to do what they were planning on doing, and give space for the jealous person to work through their own angry and jealous feelings. When a person expresses discomfort with your actions, make sure to follow these suggestions:

1- Don't argue and try to convince them that something is wrong with their thinking. Hear them out. Repeat back to them what you hear them saying.
2- Try to validate that this discussion must be difficult for them. Reflect to them your understanding of how your plan may impact them.
3- Make sure you hear them correctly. Repeat back to them the request they have of you, and the reason for the request.
4- Don't make any promises to change unless you think what they are requesting is reasonable.
5- Be compassionate that your plan may be threatening to the other individual. Just empathize with them.
6- The person feeling jealous often feels that they are losing control. Try to be understanding of their feelings.

Many people confuse jealousy with envy. So what's the difference between the two?

Jealousy	Envy
Fear of loss	Feelings of inferiority
Suspicion/anger about perceived betrayal	Longing
Low self-esteem and sadness over perceived loss	Resentment of circumstances or lacks
Uncertainty and loneliness	Ill will towards envied person (when accompanied by guilt)
Distrust	Motivation to improve
Desire to tighten the grip on the desired person	Desire to possess the attractive rival's qualities
Use of jealous feeling to manipulate	Disapproval of feelings

What if jealousy is unsubstantiated?

Jealousy can destroy a relationship, especially when it is expressed in ways that are aggressive. For example, accusations. Let's look at some examples:

Example 1: "You were flirting with her, I saw."
Example 2: "You spend money on frivolous things."
Example 3: She's five minutes late, and you start having suspicious thoughts. In an attempt to relieve your anxiety, you ask, "Where were you?" as soon as she walks through the door.

Let's look at some strategies to helping you deal with jealous feelings:

1- Admit that you're feeling jealous.
2- Express how you feel with an "I-statement."
3- Ask for more simple ways to help calm your anxious feelings. For example, "I just need to know that you still love me."
4- Journal-write through your thoughts and feelings. Answer the following questions: (a) What is this really about for me?; (b) Do I really not trust ______, or is this my way of trying to control him/her?; or (c) Does this situation remind me of a past trauma that caused my insecurities?
5- Counter your own thoughts with ones that are more reasonable.
6- Talk to a friend you trust who seems to have healthy relationships. Ask for their thoughts.
7- Review some self-talk statements – ones that are either inspirational or positive about you. (Self-esteem boosters).

Call to action: Next time you want to question someone's intentions, or accuse them, stop and ask yourself what you're trying to get accomplished, and whether accusing them is the best approach. Review the strategies above to help you through it.

Developing Healthier Relationships

What does it mean to have a healthy relationship? There are those who think a good relationship should come easily, but that's rarely the case. Arguments happen, but arguments can actually be productive and can deepen a relationship and foster trust between partners if they are handled in the right way. During the heat of the moment, however, many hurtful things can be said, creating a downward-spiral that can be more destructive than helpful. Blaming, criticizing, and put downs hurt a relationship. On the other hand, expressing pain and stating your desires and wants promote a *healthier* relationship, one with support and understanding.

In order to learn how to promote more constructive interactions, we will look at the beliefs that trigger unnecessary arguments, and learn to identify what is at the core of most arguments.

1- healthy versus unhealthy beliefs around relationships and other important areas.
2- what's at the core of the argument

What are beliefs?
In Cognitive Behavioral Psychology, beliefs are what you've learned about yourself, others, and the world from your surroundings, such as family, friends, school, work or the media. We learn through our experiences, as well as through information people have shared with us.

For example, Tara's mother has often told her daughter, "All men cheat." As a result of this teaching, Tara interrogates every man she dates because of her suspicions about their potential infidelity, even when there's no basis for her beliefs. With this viewpoint, we can see how most of her relationships are doomed from the start. Her beliefs will continue to destroy her relationships unless she *changes* them.

What are some views you hold about others that seem to be impacting your relationships negatively? Circle the *unhealthy* beliefs that resonate most, and review the Healthier View (HV) for each negative belief.

1- Their needs come before mine. ("Caretaker")
   HV: It's important to pay attention to my needs so that I can be there for others.

2- It's their duty to do _____, ______ and ______.
   HV: Though others commit to certain roles and tasks, that commitment can change over time. I need to be more flexible and understanding about these changes.

3- People are not to be trusted. Everyone has an agenda.
   HV: Trust is developed over time. People will make mistakes, and I can trust that I can work through problems with them.

4- S/he is going to leave me. (Unfounded belief).
HV: S/he has never said they will leave. S/he's been with me for a while. "People leaving me" is my own fear that I developed from my upbringing.

5- It's better to stay in the relationship for the sake of the children. I can handle the abuse.
HV: Staying in an abusive relationship will only endanger my children. I need to protect them and myself, and create a safe environment for all of us.

6- Others have to start the process of conflict resolution and apologize when it's their fault.
HV: It's just as much my responsibility as the responsibility of others to start the resolution process. Otherwise, we may never resolve the argument, causing resentments to grow.

7- If we argue, it must mean we don't have a good relationship.
HV: All relationships have conflicts; the success depends on how disagreements are handled. This involves respect, great communication, and good listening skills.

8- If there's a conflict, then it may get out of hand. It's better not to say anything.
HV: If I keep things to myself, I will have resentment. It's better for the relationship if we use effective communication skills and discuss anything that's bothering us.

9- My partner should not look at others -- ever.
HV: It's only natural that men look at other women, and vice versa. I understand that I may feel a bit insecure around that, but it's my own issue, not theirs to change.

10- Good relationships should come naturally.
HV: All relationships need work. Disagreements are okay. People have differences, and they are survivable. At times, my relationship may need more work than at other times.

What's at the core of most arguments?

It's challenging to try to discover what an argument is really about, so you have to take the time and identify what is actually happening. For example, are you arguing about the dishes not being washed in a timely manner, or are you upset because you need to know that what you say matters. Every individual has certain needs. Some of the general basic needs within a relationship include:

1- I want to know you still love me. (need to be loved)
2- I want to know that you still desire me. (need to be admired and desired)
3- I want to know that what I have to say is important. (need to be important)
4- I want to know that I will be heard. (need to be heard).
5- I want to know that you're not going to leave me. (need for security)
6- I want to know that you're not going to hurt me. (need for safety)

Think of the last time you were in an argument, and try to identify which of the above-mentioned needs felt jeopardized. For example, your partner joined a new social club and you began to worry about him/her being away from you for long periods of time. Your need for security may feel jeopardized since you fear that s/he will leave you. Instead of arguing about the social club, it's better to address your true fears and say, "I worry you're going to forget about me, and focus on the club. I just want to know that you will still want to be with me."

CALL TO ACTION: (1) List your own unhealthy beliefs, and provide a healthier view (HV) for each.

(2) Next time you argue, identify what's at the core and express your fear and need.

Understanding Codependency

Codependency involves two dysfunctional people getting worse together in an enmeshed relationship. The codependent person relies on another to help reduce their own emotional pain since they have difficulty self-regulating their own emotions. When they realize that the other person can't come through for them, they think, "I don't have anyone who really cares about me," and they feel disappointed. Anytime we adapt to the dysfunction of another, we are acting dysfunctional: "I'm only needed when you're sick."

Though codependent people can be giving, thoughtful, and helpful, they are also struggling with a need to control and manipulate those around them. They may have grown up depending on someone who was not dependable – someone who, in turn, may have been depending on something else, such as drugs or alcohol. As a result, the *then* child learned to take on the roles of both caretaker and/or enabler – and they are still doing it in their adult relationships.

Codependence is the absence of a good relationship with the *self*. Codependents allow other people to define them. The codependent person waits to see how others are feeling and thinking in order to decide how to respond. They ignore their own needs and emotions since they are disconnected from themselves. This leads to feelings of resentment. Their sense of self is not really secure, and they overreact to situations. Subsequently, they feel let down when they realize that they can't control the other person's mood. They may live with the false belief that the bad feelings they experience will dissipate if they can just win the approval of certain important people in their lives. They believe that approval is what is necessary to be happy.

Let's review some unhealthy beliefs related to Codependency.

Unhealthy Beliefs for Codependency

1. I don't let go of destructive relationships because I fear I can't handle the pain.
2. I take on your opinions and values, and put mine aside.
3. Your happiness is more important than mine. If you're happy, then I'm happy.
4. I feel good only when I know those around me like me and approve of me.
5. I make assumptions rather than verify whether or not something is true.
6. I put aside my interests, hobbies, and friends, to get closer to you.
7. My fear of confrontation dictates whether I speak up.
8. If I say "No" you will not like me and may reject me.
9. If I am there for you, and do favors for you, then you will reciprocate.
10. It's my partner's job to take care of me, and my job to take care of them.
11. I neglect my own needs and wants because I focus on taking care of others.
12. If I ask you to change, and you love me, you will change your behavior.
13. We are a reflection of each other, and therefore need to accommodate one another's requests, including requests about appearance.
14. I let you define what my behavior means.
15. I hold you responsible for my emotions: "You made me angry."

16. I work hard at protecting and pleasing you so that you will do things my way, too.

MESSAGES LEARNED

People form beliefs about what's appropriate and not appropriate through daily interactions. Messages are learned in various ways, including what is witnessed in various situations and interactions. We also form beliefs because of comments we hear from friends and family members. From these messages, people learn what they should or should not be doing. The following are common messages learned within co-dependent families.

1. **It's selfish to take care of yourself.** You were taught to think of others before yourself, and that others' needs are more important than yours. *Consequently, you may feel resentful because you neglect your own needs while taking care of others.*
2. **Don't confront and rock the boat.** You learned that if something is bothering you, to deal with it on your own. Don't risk bringing up concerns since it will disrupt the family dynamic, and people won't be able to handle it. *As a result, you learn that arguments are unhealthy and scary, and keep quiet.*
3. **Change is scary.** Co-dependent family members do what they can to keep the system from experiencing changes. *The result is experiencing the fear of change and discomfort with other people changing.*
4. **Non-Assertive communication is the norm.** In co-dependent families, it's common to show emotions rather than express them. In place of your mother telling you that she's upset with you, she yells at you and puts you down. *Consequently, you don't have the proper tools to express yourself respectfully and be heard.*

HOW CAN YOU TELL IF YOU'RE CO-DEPENDENT?

1. If you're having trouble getting your own needs met.
2. If you're not expressing your feelings and thoughts because of your fear of disappointing or upsetting a family member.
3. If you're trying to change someone's opinion of you because you have a strong need to be liked and accepted.
4. If you hold others responsible for your feelings and actions.
5. If you spend a lot of time trying to please others rather than yourself.

I'M CODEPENDENT, NOW WHAT?

1. The first step is to identify your co-dependent traits.
2. List and explore the messages you've learned from your upbringing.
3. Accept that you cannot control and change others. Learn to accept them as they are, and cope with the unwanted emotions that are triggered from others.
4. Prioritize yourself. Determine your own wants and needs and start to express them.
5. Reintegration – embrace yourself, and learn to be *self*-compassionate.

Styles of Relating: Self-Protective, Interdependent, Co-dependent

Do you ever notice yourself having similar interactions with different people? We all have a relating style. Western culture values interdependence as a relating style. Here in the U.S. we are encouraged to have at least some of our own work, friends, and hobbies that are separate from our partners' and families'. Asian and Middle Eastern cultures value codependence. The needs of the family/partner are placed above those of the individual. Where do you see your relationships on the chart below? (The shared areas of the circles represent the amount of time spent together, thinking of one another, and your general level of influence over one another.)

SELF-PROTECTIVE
(too many boundaries)

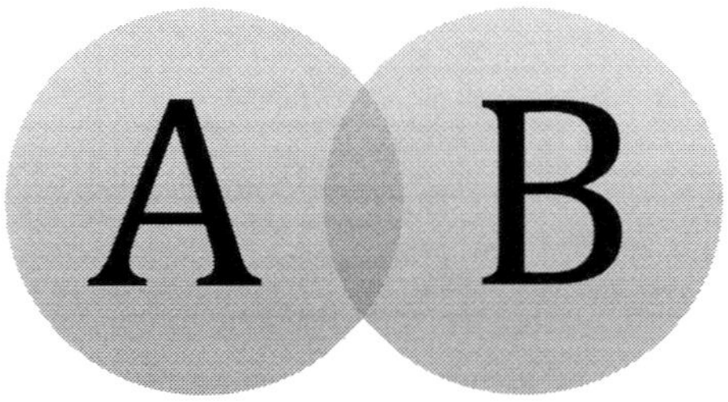

Advantages	Disadvantages
Able to care for themselves and don't appear to need others	Lonely
They see themselves as independent	Disconnected
Don't appear concerned about infidelity or being left	Creates distance within relationship
Display less fear / anxiety / pain / hurt	Emotionally guarded – lack of trust

CODEPENDENT
(too few boundaries)

Passionate and connected	Volatile
"Situationally" reliable	Disrespectful
Feel wanted and loved	Shame/ Guilt
Lots of excitement	Insecurities / distrust of partner
	Usually drugs/ addictions
	Obsessiveness / clinginess

INTERDEPENDENT
(healthy boundaries)

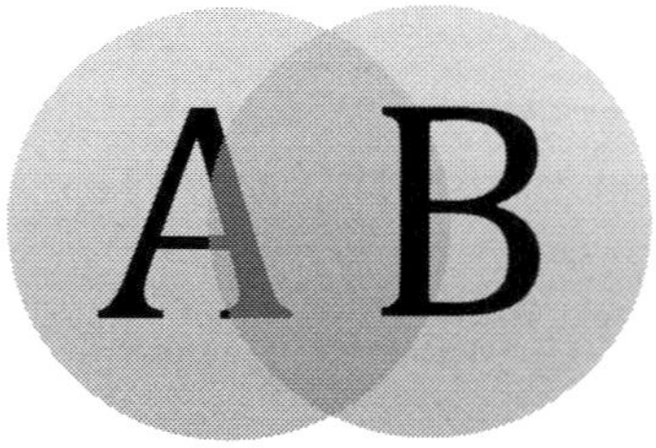

Healthy	Out of sync with certain cultures
Respectful relationship	Can be perceived as boring for those who are co-dependent
Trusting	Not as passionate as co-dependent
Confident	
Reliable and Stable	
Resolve conflicts well	

Self-Protective vs. Codependent vs. Interdependent

Understanding Boundaries

We often hear that someone lacks *boundaries*, but we may not always know what that means, because the term "boundaries" can be used in many different ways.

First let's look at defining *boundaries*; then let's understand the different types of boundaries; and finally, let's review some examples of boundaries in different situations.

Definition of Boundaries

Just as countries have borders separating one from the other, human beings have both physical and psychological ways of separating themselves from one another. Not only are we each self-contained within our own skin, with different comfort levels around personal space, but we also develop ways of letting the world know psychologically what's "me" and what's "not me". Our boundaries set rules about how much others can invade our "space", both physical and mental.

Emotional boundaries help us to feel safe. Healthy emotional boundaries prevent others from harming us or causing us to feel uncomfortable. Good boundaries are the result of knowing what we like and don't like, what we seek or avoid, and what attracts or repels us. In order to set healthy boundaries, we must develop an understanding of ourselves; we must know "who we are" and "who we are not". The better we know ourselves, the stronger our boundaries will be.

Learned in Childhood

Boundaries are learned in childhood from our parents, care-givers, family members, friends, teachers, and the like. However, sometimes the very people charged with helping us learn how to protect ourselves by developing healthy boundaries end up violating our boundaries and we don't develop a "sense of self." This negatively colors future interactions with people around us. Most significantly, it impacts our choices of mates and how we interact with them. Perhaps you can recall a childhood event involving a family member, friend, loved-one or neighbor in which he or she did or said something that was hurtful, yet when you spoke to them (if you were that courageous) about how their behavior affected you, they were perplexed or defensive. One reason for this kind of reaction is that the person may not have learned healthy boundaries themselves, and were merely treating you as they'd been treated. Others may have violated your boundaries due to lapsed judgment when they were drunk or high. It's also important to be aware of the impact that culture plays in developing our boundaries.

When it comes to boundaries, we are not all on the same page. Different things feel good or bad to different people.

Types of Boundaries

1- **Physical Boundaries** create enough space between you and others to provide a sense of comfort. It can be the physical space between you and another person or a group of people. For example:
   a. the distance you keep between you and other vehicles when driving
   b. the distance you keep from others in line at the grocery store
   c. the distance you keep when meeting a new person in a social situation

2- **Emotional Boundaries** draw distinctions between personal interactions that feel good and nurturing and those that feel like invasions. We have an invisible psychological shield around us, and when someone crosses that line by being dishonest, too nosey, sharing too much, or asking personal questions about sex, politics, religion or money, our boundaries feel violated. For example:
   a. Someone you recently met calls you every 10 or 15 minutes.
   b. Your partner has an affair.
   c. Your friend frequently calls and dumps on you.

3- **Intellectual Boundaries** – Our sense of self includes our good ideas, mastery of learned topics, scholarly achievements, our ability to solve problems, and even our wit. When someone dismisses these things as worthless, or fails to listen to us or appreciate our intellectual abilities, we feel angry and unvalued. For example:
   a. when someone "does your thinking for you"
   b. when someone makes decisions for you
   c. when someone takes credit for your ideas or work

4- **Sexual Boundaries** – We are (hopefully) taught that our bodies belong to us, not to anyone else, and that inappropriate sex talk, unwanted touching, or all-out sexual assaults are invasions of our boundaries. Invasions of sexual boundaries are violating both physically and psychologically, and can leave us feeling extremely vulnerable. For example:
   a. Sexual harassment
   b. Being manipulated into doing something sexual
   c. Rape

5- **Financial Boundaries** – Money - a symbol of power - can protect us from adversity, as well as protect loved-ones. Therefore, when our money is abused, misused or stolen, our power to protect ourselves and others is threatened. For example:
   a. money taken from a shared bank account without your knowledge
   b. money borrowed and not returned
   c. financial promises broken

Potential Boundary Violations

Workplace	• Speaking in a different language while other coworkers are present • Eating foods with an overpowering odor at the work desk (fish, garlic, etc) • Holding side conversations during meetings
Home	• Entering another person's room without knocking • Rifling through another's personal belongings • Changing the television channel without asking family members if it's okay
Friends	• Not keeping your friend's information confidential • Providing excessive favors, or requesting too many favors • Showing up late to a scheduled meeting
Acquiantances	• Revealing too much information (TMI) about yourself • Showing up late to scheduled meetings • Not responding to emails and phone calls
Community	• Using your cell phone in a movie theater • Not letting someone merge into traffic • Playing loud music after midnight (car or home)
Self	• Eating too much or too little • Engaging in unsafe sex • Having difficulty saying no

Healthy Boundaries

We create healthy boundaries to feel that our identities are safe within our surroundings. They help us set limits so that we form supportive relationships. Healthy boundaries are flexible so that we can foster nurturing relationships and let go of those that are harmful. Boundaries can be relaxed or more structured, depending on the situation. Healthy boundaries help us work through conflicts. Good boundaries help us decipher whether someone is taking advantage of us or not.

Problematic Boundaries

When we set too many boundaries, we are keeping people at a distance and not developing healthy relationships. Consequently, relationships don't last as long. People with too many boundaries (walled-in) tend to feel isolated and lonely. They distrust people. On the other hand, people who don't have enough boundaries (boundaryless) trust too easily, give too much, have difficulty saying "No" to requests, and stay in relationships longer than they want, including ones that are harmful to them. Either extreme is unhealthy.

Summary

It is important to set healthy personal boundaries. Without them, you are vulnerable to people who have no idea what your wants and needs are. The way to set healthy boundaries is to develop awareness of what feels good to you and what feels bad. Once you know your boundaries, you can (assertively) communicate your preferences to others, which is an essential part of being a mature, healthy, functional adult.

How are Your Boundaries?

	Mark the appropriate level of response to each question.	0- Never	1- Rarely	2- Sometimes	3- Often	
1	Does giving to others make you end up feeling overwhelmed?					
2	Do you feel as though others are trying to run your life?					
3	Do you say "yes" when really you want to say "no"?					
4	If you say yes to something you don't want to do, do you feel resentful?					
5	Do you say "yes" because you don't want to deal with confrontation?					
6	Do you say "yes" because you worry about people not liking you, leaving you, or disapproving of you?					
7	Do you try to keep those around you happy?					
8	Do you feel guilty when saying "no" to someone?					
9	Do you think your own feelings and needs don't matter?					
10	Would you do mostly anything to avoid hurting others?					
11	Do you feel that you are never caught up with daily tasks, as if your life isn't your own?					
12	Do you feel taken advantage of by those close to you?					
13	Do you see yourself as the only one who can help?					
14	Is it difficult for you to disappoint others?					
15	If someone criticizes you, do you automatically believe their criticism is true?					
16	Do you let others define what your behavior means?					
17	Do you give too much in a friendship or intimate relationship?					
18	Do you trust too easily?					
19	Do you get overinvolved with the problems of other people?					
20	Do you worry about intruding on others?					
21	Do you get involved too quickly?					
22	Do you stay in relationships longer than you're interested?					
23	Is it difficult for you to let go of a relationship that is destructive?					
24	Do you have difficulty with keeping yourself on track with personal goals (eating healthier, not smoking, drinking or using)?					
	Add All the Columns, then place the sum into the right box.					

Less Than 24: You probably have good healthy boundaries / **24-48:** Boundaries may be a little weak, could use some strengthening / **49-72:** Boundaries are fairly weak. It's time to learn to set some boundaries.

Setting Boundaries

We face requests on a daily basis. Sometimes it's easy to set boundaries; other times it's not. When we give too much, we risk becoming overwhelmed and resentful -- and then guess what? We get upset with those around us and feel taken advantage of. Instead of seeing it as *our* responsibility to set the boundary, we may see it as the responsibility of the other person to not make requests.

Angry people often give too much, yet if they simply start learning to set proper limits, and pay attention to their own needs, they may end up not getting so upset.

Though it may seem as though saying "No" should be easy, for those accustomed to feeling responsible for taking care of others, saying "No" is a tough thing to do. So let's look at some strategies to set boundaries with other people.

4 Steps to Setting Boundaries with Others

1- Acknowledge that you heard the request. Repeat what they're asking from you, and if needed, seek further clarification.
2- Evaluate whether or not the request is something you would like to fulfill, or would you prefer to forego it?
3- Inform the person whether or not you'll be able to fulfill the request. If you choose not to, it's important that you don't apologize for it. You're simply explaining your reason. Be honest with your response, you don't need to come up with excuses.
4- Say "Yes" or "No". Stating "No" is a way of setting limits. For example, "It's not something I want to do."

For example: "I understand that you would like me to take you to the airport tomorrow. I won't be able to since I'm on a time deadline with my projects." Some people may find it rude to say "No" and their guilt feelings become overwhelming. If this happens to you, be sure to process your emotions during this time of trying to change. Talk to your counselor to get some guidance. Someone who is very giving may put aside their work in order to drive their friend to the airport. But at a later date, if they request a favor of that same friend and the friend says they cannot do it, it can lead to frustration and resentment.

You will have to decide how insistent your response needs to be in a given situation. For example, if someone has been drinking and they plan to drive you home, it's okay to be insistent and say, "It is not okay that you drive the car. You need to give me the keys."

Sometimes people find it challenging to be completely honest when setting limits because they feel they're sounding harsh or too rigid. You could soften what you're saying with your tone of voice and choice of words. Using the same example above, you could say, "I would love it if I could be the driver on the way home. They have checkpoints out there tonight, and I would hate to see you get a DUI."

Boundaries with Self

Though we have been focusing on setting boundaries with others, it is also important to set limits for yourself. For example, you want to start living a healthier lifestyle, but you continue to consume chocolate and unhealthy snacks. For some, it's more difficult to set limits with oneself that it is with others.

Boundaries with the Community

When someone cuts in front of you while you're standing in line, do you say anything? If you see a parent physically abusing their child in public, do you say or do anything? While waiting in the doctor's office, do you use your cell phone to make calls, even though there are signs not to use your phone?

Helpful tips in setting limits

1- Be confident when setting limits – you have the right to say "No." You don't have to come up with excuses as to why you cannot fulfill a request. You can say, "It's not something I'm interested in doing." No one can argue that you are interested in doing something! It may bother them that I'm not pleasing them, but be okay with that.
2- It's also okay to say, "I have other plans." That's not a lie because your "plan" could be to stay home, relax and watch TV.
3- Don't apologize for saying "No." Keep reminding yourself that it's your right.
4- Take your time in coming up with your response. It's reasonable to ask for time to decide. Evaluate whether it's something you want to do or not.
5- If you're not okay with fulfilling the other person's complete request, then share what part of the request you might be willing to fulfill.

When is it a good time to set limits?

1- When you're taking care of others more than yourself.
2- When you're asked to share more about yourself than you feel comfortable disclosing.
3- When you're asked to do something that goes against your values.
4- Simply when you don't want to do something.
5- When you start feeling depleted because you are giving so much.
6- When you're doing all the work within the relationship.

It's okay to express your wants and needs. Here are some formats you could use:
I would like for you to _______ ; or, I don't like when you _______.

If you're uncomfortable with something, you could use the following: *I feel uncomfortable when you _________ (specific behavior). Or, Please stop _______.*

Exercise 1 - Practice setting limits when asked to fulfill a request

Let's put these skills into practice.

Think of situations that involve a *request or a favor*, and list them below:

1. ____
2. ____
3. ____

Using the 4 steps, write how you would go about setting limits.

1- Acknowledge that you heard the request.
2- Evaluate whether or not the request is something you would like to fulfill.
3- Inform the person whether or not you can fulfill the request.
4- Say "Yes" or "No."

For example: I understand that you want me to lend you money. It's not something I can do at this time.

Situation 1: ____

Situation 2: ____

Situation 3: ____

Exercise 2 – Practice setting limits when you're uncomfortable

Think of situations that were *uncomfortable* for you. List them below.

1. ____
2. ____
3. ____

Next, either express your wants and needs, or express your discomfort. For example, *I feel uncomfortable when you sit too close to me.*

Situation 1: ____

Situation 2: ____

Situation 3: ____

CALL TO ACTION: Practice setting limits.

Some contents adapted from Matthew McKay, PhD and Peter Rogers, Ph.D. from the Anger Control Workbook

Stressors, and How They Impact You Behaviorally, Cognitively, and Emotionally

Today we're going to talk about stressors. Stressors are proportional to anger. That means that the more stress you experience, the greater the likelihood you'll feel angry. A stressor is *any* change, whether it's a good change or a bad one. Planning a wedding can be a stressor, just as much as having your car stolen is a stressor.

On the lines below, list all the stressors in your life.

____

____

____

____

Now let's look at how our stressors impact us. They impact us in four different ways: behaviorally, cognitively, emotionally, and physically. Stressors can affect us behaviorally, for example, by contributing to the impulse to overeat, drink alcohol, or smoke cigarettes. Stressors can affect us cognitively by contributing to negative thoughts, such as: "I can't handle this", "I won't get through this", or "No one will help me." We can experience depression, anger, apathy, impatience, or low self-esteem due to emotional stressors. Finally, stressors can impact us physically by contributing to fatigue, chest pain, muscle tightness, headaches, and high blood pressure. We are focusing on these four areas, however there are other areas, such as spirituality, that can be impacted by stressors.

When you notice any of the above symptoms, it's important to realize that they are signs you are under stress and that you need to do something to address the tension. The following is a visual depiction of how stress escalates over time.

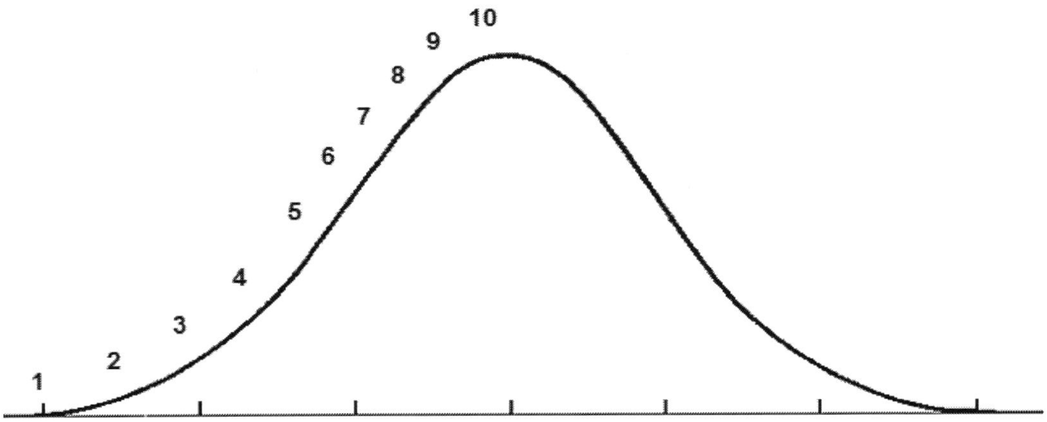

As the numbers increase, the severity of the symptoms will also increase. For example, at a 2 you might experience a slight tightness in your neck. If you ignore the tightness when it's at a 2, tomorrow you may be at a 4, and if you continue to ignore it, the following day you may not be able to get out of bed. The goal is to learn to address your tight neck when it's at a 2, even though we may be tempted to ignore it because it isn't yet severe. We're here to manage our anger, and the best way to do that is to prevent it. By taking steps to address stress symptoms right away - when they are at a 1 or 2 instead of a 6 or 7 – we increase the chances of regulating our anger. That gets much harder to do at the higher numbers.

What are the telltale signs that *you* are experiencing stress? Rate the severity of your stress based on your symptoms. For example, at a 2, I start to become forgetful. At a 6, I will eat four bags of cookies, etc.

Level 2-4 Stress Symptoms:

____

Level 5-7 Stress Symptoms:

____

Level 8-10 Stress Symptoms:

____

Stress symptoms at level 2-4 are easiest to manage.
Stress symptoms at level 5-7 are more difficult to manage.
Stress symptoms at level 8-10 put you in the danger zone.

Don't ignore low level stress symptoms! DO SOMETHING ABOUT THEM....

Tips for Stress Management

The word *stress* was coined by Hans Selye, a pioneer endocrinologist who conducted scientific work on the subject. Selye defined stress as "the non-specific response of the body to any demand for change." *Stress* is what we experience when something poses a challenge to our well-being, whereas a *stressor* is the stimulus that triggers the stress. Why is managing your stress so important? If you don't take care of yourself, stress can lead to major health problems. Though some stress is good for us, too much stress can be overwhelming and debilitating. If you carry too much stress and don't deal with it properly, you risk acting out with behaviors such as snapping at those around you. It's normal to feel some stress, but when your level is over a 5 based on a scale of 1-10, it's important to reduce it to a level that is more manageable for you. The following is a list of stress management tips:

1. **TAKE BREAKS:** Schedule some breaks and replenish your energy. Take a nap to feel refreshed.
2. **STAY HYDRATED:** Keep your body hydrated. Drink lots of water, sometimes tea.
3. **STAY CLEAR OF SUBSTANCES:** Refrain from using drugs or alcohol.
4. **EXPLORE YOUR STRESSORS:** Identify what's triggering your stress. Awareness is important so that you can do something about it if you choose to do so.
5. **CHECK YOUR THOUGHTS:** Counter negative thoughts and focus on those that will help you through a stressful situation. Negative thoughts impact stress levels.
6. **PRIORITIZE & ORGANIZE:** Make a list of what needs to get done, and work towards the items that need immediate attention. Plan to complete less important tasks at a later time.
7. **TIME MANAGEMENT:** Schedule tasks several weeks in advance. Block out times within the week to accomplish some tasks. Set boundaries when possible. Delegate tasks when possible.
8. **BREATHING EXERCISES:** Allot several times throughout the day to practice deep breathing.
9. **LAUGHTER & FUN:** Laugh and have fun. Humor is a great way to help reduce stress.
10. **JOURNAL WRITING:** Journal writing is a safe means to process stressors.
11. **PROBLEM SOLVING:** Identify triggers and problem-solve them. It helps them to seem more manageable.
12. **FORGIVE:** Holding a grudge carries a lot of heavy and negative energy with it. Learn to forgive to release the burden.
13. **SEEKING SUPPORT:** Ask for help. Inform your friends and family members that you want their emotional support. Set some time to talk to them.
14. **COMMUNICATE:** Express your concerns to people when it's fitting and appropriate. Holding onto your frustrations will lead to more stress and worry.

15. **STRETCH & TENSION RELEASE:** Practice some tension releasing exercises. Make sure to take some stretch breaks; it helps to reboot your body and mind.

16. **EXERCISE:** Walk, jog, hike, or do any exercise you find helpful. Exercising will help release endorphins and dopamine, which help reduce levels of stress. Plus, your health will be better.

17. **EATING:** During times of stress, people either eat more or less. Be sure that your diet is well-balanced. Snack on healthy foods. Keep the fat and caffeine in your diet at a minimum.

18. **WHAT'S IN YOUR CONTROL:** Focus on the tasks that you can change rather than the ones you cannot control. Learn to accept what you have, and let go of the things you cannot change.

19. **SET BOUNDARIES:** Take your time before responding to requests. In place of saying "Yes," think about what's involved with the task, and examine whether you can realistically take on the responsibility.

20. **ENGAGE IN THE ARTS:** Engage in artistic and creative pursuits such as poetry, painting, or reading a book.

21. **POSITIVE SELF TALK:** Create and review a list of positive statements about yourself and your life.

22. **MEDITATE:** Once a day sit quietly and clear out your mind in silence.

23. **DO SOMETHING YOU ENJOY:** Read a book, watch a movie, or do what you consider a hobby.

24. **FUN ACTIVITY:** See some friends. Try a fun activity.

25. **INSPIRATION:** Surround yourself with inspiring photos and quotes.

26. **GRATITUDE:** List everything you feel gratitude for and review it several times.

27. **APPEARANCE:** Wear your attractive clothes. Bathe and groom yourself to feel better.

28. **WARM BATH:** Take a warm bath or shower to relax.

29. **DELEGATE:** Delegate tasks that can be delegated so that you can focus on your most important areas.

30. **GET SUNLIGHT:** Go outside in nature and get some vitamin D.

31. **VITAMINS:** Take vitamins that provide nourishment and energy.

32. **RESIST:** Resist the urge to be productive all the time.

33. **LIMIT TELEVISION:** This is usually a pass-time that is not enjoyable. You want to work towards connecting with yourself, not disconnecting.

34. **GET PAMPERED:** Get a massage, manicure, facial, or pamper yourself in some other way.

CALL TO ACTION: Select your favorite stress management tips, and incorporate them this week.

Problem Solving Skills to Help with Managing Stress

In this day and age, stress levels are at an all-time high. We have so much on our plates -- including stressors around work, family, finances and responsibilities. Technology, instead of providing us with some down time, has actually given us more to learn and more to do, which can result in less relaxation and less sleep. When your life begins to feel unmanageable, start paying attention to your stressors. Instead of ignoring what needs to be addressed, write it down, get clear on it, and problem-solve your way through it.

The purpose of learning problem solving skills is to help you feel that you have a better handle on your life. Once you complete this worksheet, you will have an action item: something you can actually *do* about your stressors rather than feel overwhelmed and avoid them. Remember, a stressor is any change (positive *or* negative) that causes stress. For example, getting married is a happy event yet trying to organize a wedding day and all that goes along with it can be very stressful.

In this next section, list your current stressors:

1.	5.	9.	13.
2.	6.	10.	14.
3.	7.	11.	15.
4.	8.	12.	16.

From the list above, circle the ones you can actually change, and place a square around the ones you think you can't do anything about.

From the items you circled, select a stressor you would like to start problem-solving now. List the item in the problem solving section "A" below. From the items you cannot change (those with a square), select the one that you would like to emotionally work through, and list it in "A" under the section that reads "Being Compassionate."

Problem Solving

A. What's the problem or stressor?

____

B. What would you like? What's your goal? (Hint: Usually the goal is the opposite of the problem):

____

C. List three possible solutions. Be sure not to evaluate them; you will do that in another step. (Helpful hint: Don't judge your responses as you write them. List any ideas that come to mind).

1. ______________________________

2. ______________________________

3. ______________________________

D. Evaluate each option above by listing both advantages and disadvantages.

Option 1: ______________________________

Advantages	Disadvantages
1.	1.
2.	2.

Option 2: ______________________________

Advantages	Disadvantages
1.	1.
2.	2.

Option 3: ______________________________

Advantages	Disadvantages
1.	1.
2.	2.

E. Select the option of preference and create an action plan. (Your action plan includes your goal for this week)

____

____

____

____

Being Compassionate

A. What's the problem or stressor?

____

B. What would you like? What's your goal? (Hint: usually the goal is the opposite of the problem):

____

C. List three possible ways you could deal with your discomfort and evaluate them within the boxes below. Some examples include journal writing, talking to a friend, talking to your therapist, engaging in a relaxing activity, and getting a massage.

Option 1:

____

Advantages	Disadvantages
1.	1.
2.	2.

Option 2:

____

Advantages	Disadvantages
1.	1.
2.	2.

Option 3:

____

Advantages	Disadvantages
1.	1.
2.	2.

D. Select the option of preference and create an action plan.

____

____

____

Oftentimes goals don't get accomplished because there are obstacles that get in the way. Think through the realistic obstacles that may get in the way of your action plan. How can you problem solve through the obstacles?

____

____

____

____

SMART GOAL SETTING - Make sure your goal is SMART.

1. **Specific** - Tells exactly what you will do.
2. **Measurable** - How will you know if you accomplished your goal?
3. **Appropriate** – It aligns with your current goals.
4. **Realistic** - Not too hard, or too easy to do.
5. **Time** - Tells when goal will be completed.

ACCOUNTABILITY

Who will you share your goal with? Can they hold you accountable? Will you inform them of your plan and share with them when you've accomplished it? This increases the likelihood of your working towards your goal.

Wheel of Life: How Satisfied are You?

When we stop paying attention to the areas in our lives that matter most, we can feel lost, unfulfilled, or out of balance. To achieve balance in our lives, it's helpful to take a bird's eye view of the areas that are important to us, such as career, health, romantic partnership, friendships, etc. From this perspective, we can assess our level of satisfaction with each one, and decide to improve our satisfaction in areas where it's lacking. Look at the figure below, and try to imagine your life as a "wheel", where your important life areas are separated by "spokes".

Step 1: Select 8 life categories that are important to you, and use them to label each "spoke." You can choose from the following list, or create your own.

1. Partner – love, relationship
2. Family – parents, children, relatives
3. Social – friends, activities
4. Job/Career – satisfaction with work, colleagues
5. Health – diet, fitness, exercise
6. Mental Health – therapy, journaling, stress management
7. Fun – happiness, interests, hobbies
8. Financial/ Money – income, savings, investments
9. Creativity – painting/drawing, music, producing, writing
10. Spirituality – meditation, religion
11. Growth – learning, education, emotional growth
12. Community – helping, volunteering

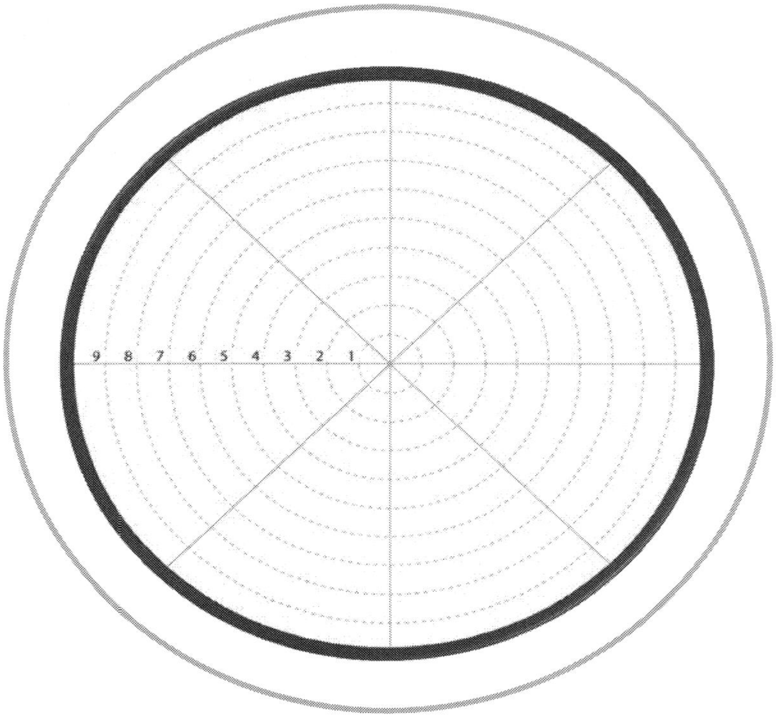

Step 2: Ask yourself how satisfied you are in each area right now, and rate your satisfaction level on a scale from 0 to 10, where zero is completely unsatisfied and 10 is the most satisfied you could be. (Note: Your level of satisfaction can change daily or weekly. Just identify *your feeling* about it. Remember, this is about how you feel, and not about how you think others see you).

Step 3: Trace the arcs that represent your ratings of 0 (middle of circle) to 10 (outer circle) in each area.

Step 4: Starting from the center of the wheel and moving outward, shade in the areas.

Step 5: On your second wheel, shade in the areas as you would like them to appear in the future. Keep in mind that our time and energy are finite. There are only so many hours in a day and days in the week. We can't be at 100% in every area at all times. So remember that when you devote more time and effort to one area, you will have to devote less to another. Be realistic!

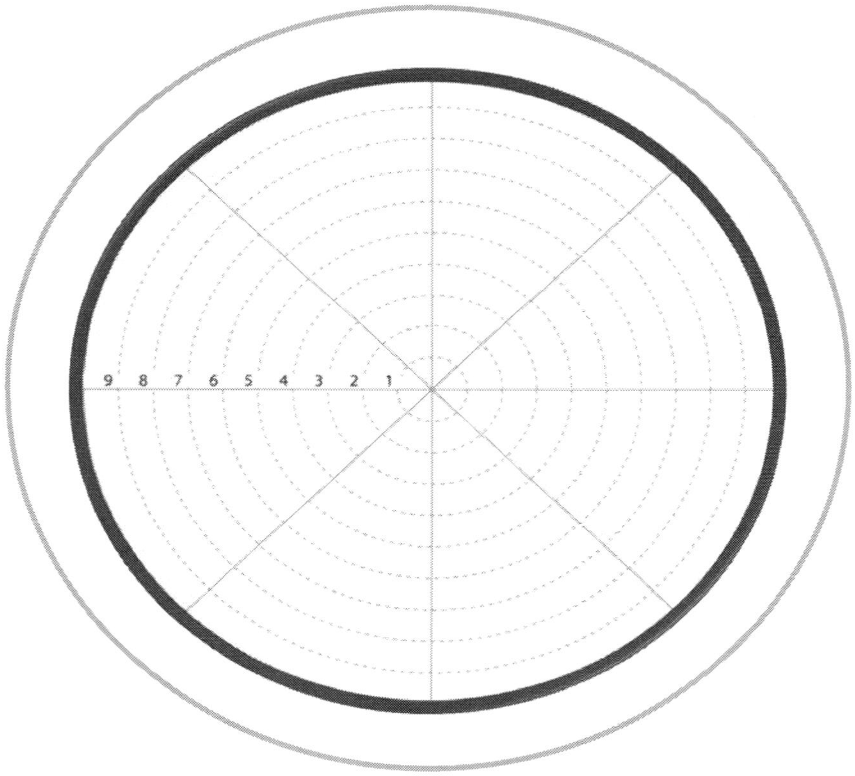

Step 6: What steps will you take to start shifting your level of satisfaction in the important areas of your life?

Step 7: What will you need to delegate or refrain from doing in order to increase overall life satisfaction?

Call to Action: Reassess how satisfied you are at a later time.

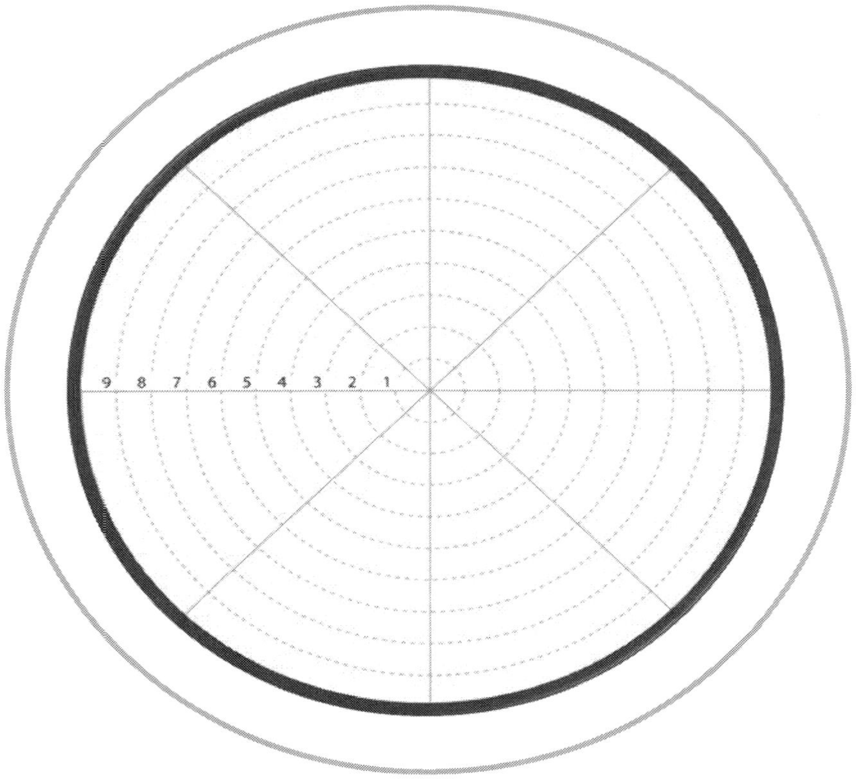

Change, Accept, & Let Go

What am I reacting to?

What's happening with me: thoughts, emotions, sensations?

What meaning am I giving it?

- Is this fact or opinion?
- Is there anything I can change about this situation, right now?
- How important is it?
- How important will it be in a year?
- What would someone else make of this?
- What would I say to a friend?
- What's the bigger picture?

What are my options?

CHANGE

- What can I change?
  - Environment
  - Situation
  - My reaction
- How can I make the changes?
- What resources do I need?
- When can I do it?
- What do I do first?

ACCEPT

- It is as it is
- I don't have to agree with it, or judge it good or bad
- I can always come back to it later
- I can keep my options open
- This is a normal body reaction
- I don't have to fight it, or try to stop it.
- It will pass

LET GO

- Is it worth it?
- Is this something I can leave or let go of, and move on from?

What can I do that will best help me/others/the situation right now?

"When we are no longer able to change a situation, we are challenged to change ourselves" Viktor Frankl

Avoidance and Escape

Most people assume that avoiding a situation means you are not really dealing with the issues or problems you have. Although this may be true, there are certain times when avoidance and escape can actually help you manage a stressful situation in a more constructive manner. Below are some examples.

THOUGHTFUL AVOIDANCE

If an event occurs and your immediate reaction to it is anger, you can decide it might be better to "sit this one out." This is a smart move if taking an angry action might put you at risk for harming someone or might cause you to suffer some kind of loss, such as a relationship or a job. This kind of avoidance is called **"thoughtful avoidance"** because temporarily avoiding a situation that angers you and coming back to it later when you are in a calmer state of mind can help you generate better solutions.

PLANNED AVOIDANCE

Another constructive way of using avoidance is called **"Planned Avoidance."** This is when you identify in advance a situation that has previously triggered anger, so you decide you'll avoid it. For example, if rush-hour traffic always gets you worked up, see if you can re-schedule your work hours to avoid the worst of it.

AVOIDANCE BY TIME DELAY

This is another way that avoidance can be helpful. For example, at work if you're asked to work on a Saturday, when you already have family plans, respond with, "Can I let you know tomorrow?" This delay will allow you to regain composure, consider the possible consequences of saying "no," consider some options, and then make that phone call with your decision in a calm, reasonable way. In another situation, somebody might make a request when you're already angry about something else. To avoid letting the anger spill over into this new situation and cause you to respond in a way you normally wouldn't, let the person know that you will have to take a moment to think about it before answering. Just this brief delay might help you come up with a better answer.

THE AVOIDANCE ADVANTAGE

Avoidance can help you communicate more effectively and get the outcome that you would like. Different situations call for different measures. For example, in a family setting, finding an alternative solution to a problem is different than finding an alternative solution in a work setting. In a family, children may misbehave and need to be disciplined. If the way you express your displeasure with children is not effective, it might be better to ask your husband or wife to deal with the situation instead, especially if you are too easily triggered into an over-angry response. In a work setting, an alternative solution when trying to communicate with a co-worker who angers or annoys you would be via e-mail, memo, or letter rather than handling it in person and saying something you'll regret. This alternative might be more effective and less risky.

ESCAPE STRATEGIES

Sometimes it's almost impossible to avoid situations which can trigger anger, so having a few escape strategies like the ones below can help you *leave* an "anger" situation that's emerging, or make a quick getaway even if you've already become angry.

1. **Time Outs:** When two people are in a heated conversation, sometimes their emotions take over and it escalates, so taking a break or a "time-out" can help them calm down and return to the conversation with cooler heads. With your partner, you can use phrases like, "I'm upset now so I'd like us to talk about something else (or go out to eat, or watch TV) for a while. We can try to talk about this later."

2. **Pre-Planned Escape:** If you know in advance that a particular meeting with someone is likely to be unpleasant and unproductive, it might make sense to limit the amount of time to be spent in that interaction. You can even say, "I just have ten minutes," or, "I can give you until my show comes on." It can help put your emotions aside and deal with the problem at hand more efficiently.

3. **Distraction:** If you keep hashing and rehashing the things that make you angry in a discussion, you only end up getting angrier. Distract yourself. Go to a bowling alley, a baseball game, or out to dinner with a family member. It's likely to put you in a better mood. Don't talk about the anger-related situations. If angry thoughts intrude during the "distraction" activity, let them pass and bring your mental focus back to the present moment. The goal of this technique is to break the rumination cycle (thinking about what makes you angry over and over again) with *competing* thoughts and activities. This lets you to step back from your anger, enjoy the distraction, and possibly come away with a new perspective.

Cognitive Behavioral Chart on Healthy Vs. Unhealthy Angry Beliefs

Unhealthy Belief	**Hurtful** Thought	**Feelings**	**Destructive** Behavior	**Consequence**
People are not to be trusted.	She called in sick on a Monday. She was probably out late last night, and didn't want to come to work today.	Angry, annoyed, exploited, and disrespected.	I questioned her. I asked whether she went to the Dr. I told her that I didn't believe her.	She never returned to work. I knew she was lying, otherwise she would have shown up. I can't trust people.
Healthy Belief	**Helpful** Thought	**Feelings**	**Constructive** Behavior	**Consequence**
It's better to be understanding and give the benefit of doubt.	She has sick days she can use. I've used sick days when I wasn't sick. Plus she may really be sick.	Comfortable, accepting, compassionate, and understanding.	When she returned to work the next day, I checked in with her to make sure she's okay. She did well with work.	I learn that by being flexible and understanding, I foster great work relationships and increased employee productivity.
Unhealthy Belief	**Hurtful** Thought	**Feelings**	**Destructive** Behavior	**Consequence**
I have to yell or be aggressive, otherwise people won't listen or do as I ask.	This waiter is stupid for not writing down our order, and I know he's going to make a mistake.	Anxious, worried that he's going to get the order wrong. Need to control the situation.	I tell the waiter that he needs to write down our order so he doesn't make a mistake; otherwise I will talk to his manager.	He feels intimidated, and as a result, messes up on the order. My family felt embarrassed by my behavior.
Healthy Belief	**Helpful** Thought	**Feelings**	**Constructive** Behavior	**Consequence**
People respond better when communication is assertive and respectful.	The waiter may be great at remembering orders. It's just my own trust issues.	I'm more comfortable with the idea that he will remember the order. It feels better to try to trust him.	I *ask* him whether he will remember the order. And I compliment him on his memory skills.	We had a nice exchange with the waiter. I enjoyed a pleasant meal with my friends.

Exercise: Try filling in the remaining boxes for the first two rows. For the last two, try working on one unhealthy belief you have, and one healthy one.

Unhealthy Belief	**Hurtful** Thought	**Feelings**	**Destructive** Behavior	**Consequence**
All men cheat.				
Healthy Belief	**Helpful** Thought	**Feelings**	**Constructive** Behavior	**Consequence**
I am loveable.				
Unhealthy Belief	**Hurtful** Thought	**Feelings**	**Destructive** Behavior	**Consequence**
Healthy Belief	**Helpful** Thought	**Feelings**	**Constructive** Behavior	**Consequence**

Self-Defeating vs. Self-Enhancing Thoughts and Behaviors

Cognitive-Behavioral Theory suggests that thoughts precede emotions and emotions precede behavior. Thus, if we can become aware of our thoughts, we can increase control over our emotions, and ultimately be in the driver's seat where our behavior is concerned.

Self-Defeating Thoughts

Self-defeating (SD) thoughts are thinking patterns that negatively impact our mood. In essence, they are skewed and irrational ways of looking at ourselves and the world around us. The following list includes negative thinking styles, along with their alternative, rational, self-enhancing (SE) styles of thinking.

1. **(SD) Polarized Thinking**: Things are black or white, good or bad, perfect or utter failures, with no middle ground. ("My mother was a horrible person.")
   (SE) Gray Area Thinking: Two or more things can be true at the same time. ("My mother was very cold and emotionally distant when I was growing up. AND she used to take me for ice cream on Saturdays.")

2. **(SD) Overgeneralization**: You use words like "always" or "never" to describe yourself or the world around you. You declare a single, negative event as evidence of a never-ending pattern. ("You never help me.")
   (SE) Identifying Single Events: Identifying an event as a singular occurrence. Instead of saying, "You never help me," try saying, "Last night you didn't help me with the dishes. ***I would like*** for you to help me with them."

3. **(SD) Catastrophizing/Magnifying**: You blow things out of proportion – make a mountain out of a molehill. ("I failed my English midterm. Now I won't graduate from college!"
   (SE) Stepping Out-Of-The-Mind: Observing, as a detached witness, what is actually happening around you, and then taking the necessary steps to rectify the situation. ("If I study hard, I can pass the final.")
   (SD) Expecting Disaster: "What if tragedy strikes? What if it happens to me?"
   (SE) Looking at the Data: "It's terrible what happened to her, but the chances of that happening in general are very low."

4. **(SD) Blaming:** You hold other people responsible for your problems. Or, you go to the opposite extreme and blame yourself for everything bad that happens.
   (SE) Re-Attributing: Identifying the internal factors in ourselves or the external factors in others that actually cause the problem. Then, shifting focus to resolutions.

5. **(SD) "Should"-ing**: You have a list of ironclad rules about how you and others should act. When people break these "rules", you become very angry. Also, when you violate these rules yourself, you feel extremely guilty.

(SE) Having Realistic Expectations: Acknowledging that we are humans - not machines – allows us to have more moderate expectations of ourselves and others. *Assume* your rules will be broken sometimes. *Expect* someone to cut you off on the highway.

6. **(SD) Mental Filter**: You focus on a small, negative detail of a particular event or situation and are blind to the positive aspects of it. This is like focusing on a tiny drop of black ink floating in a large bathtub of clear water. ("I forgot one of my lines tonight. I gave a horrible performance."
   (SE): Rating on a Scale from 1-10: Acknowledging there is a range of possible levels of "success" and "failure". ("The audience loved the show and I only forgot one line!")

7. **(SD) Discounting the Positive**: Seeing positive experiences as "flukes", insisting they "don't count", and downplaying their significance.
   (SE) Cost-Benefit Analyzing: Listing the advantages and disadvantages of pessimistic thinking shows us what we gain and lose from thought distortions. The unbalanced list will guide you in choosing the most profitable thinking style.

8. **(SD) Minimizing the Negative: (**opposite of magnifying) Denying and rationalizing wrong-doings when confronted with irrefutable facts. Using reduction words and phrases such as "barely," "once," "no big deal," "only a little," or "all I did was."
   (SE) Taking Responsibility: Acknowledging all aspects of a situation, including your own behavior.

9. **(SD) Emotional Reasoning**- Assuming that your negative emotions reflect the way things really are simply because you feel them: "I am terrified of flying. Airplanes must be very dangerous."
   (SE) Surveying: Asking others whether our thoughts and attitudes are realistic**.**

10. **(SD) Labeling**: Labeling is an extreme form of all-or-nothing thinking. Instead of simply identifying what happened: "I made a mistake," you attach an overly generalized, negative label to yourself: "I'm a loser." When labeling others, it's a form of verbal abuse.
    (SE) Defining: Examining the *meaning* of a label such as "loser" will reveal that it represents specific behaviors, not the total person.

11. **(SD) Jumping to Conclusions**: You make negative assumptions without evidence to support them.
    - **Mind Reading**: You decide what people are feeling and why they act the way they do. In particular, you assume how others feel about you.
    - **Fortune Telling**: You predict that things will turn out badly, even when past history is evidence to the contrary.

    (SE) Examining the Evidence: Looking for the existence or lack thereof of experiences that prove/disprove our assumptions.

Self-Defeating Behaviors

Self-defeating (SD) behaviors are those that negatively impact our physical well-being. The following is a list of self-defeating behaviors:

1. Alcohol/Substance/Prescription Medication Abuse / Smoking
2. Watching excessive television (i.e. more than 4 hours every night)
3. Emotional eating / binge eating / starving oneself
4. Driving dangerously / placing others at risk
5. Nail/cuticle-biting
6. Hair-pulling
7. Cutting/ self-mutilation/ skin-picking
8. Breaking things in anger
9. Excessive sex/ unprotected sex with multiple partners
10. Internet addictions
11. Excessive exercise / Being sedentary
12. Spending excessively
13. Gambling
14. Isolating
15. Negative self-talk

Self-Enhancing Behaviors

Self-Enhancing (SE) behaviors are those that positively impact our physical well-being. Keep in mind that the goal is finding a balance. The following is a list of self-enhancing behaviors:

1. Exercising
2. Yoga/ Breath work
3. Meditation/Relaxation/Visualization
4. Taking vacations
5. Talking to friends/ therapists
6. Journal Writing
7. Bubble baths
8. Going to the beach/Being in nature
9. Health Management/ Routine doctors' visits
10. Hobbies such as Painting/Singing/Poetry/Reading
11. Positive self-talk
12. Taking breaks

Testing Unhealthy Beliefs

About Beliefs

In Cognitive Behavioral Psychology, beliefs are what you learned about yourself, others and the world through your surroundings such as family, friends, school, work, or the media. We learn from our experiences, as well as through information that people have shared with us. The good news is that the beliefs that result in destructive behavior and uncomfortable feelings are learned, so they can be unlearned. When replacing an unhealthy belief with one that is more helpful, you experience a shift in your mood and attitude; your faulty perception of a situation can change. Your improved insight into the underlying thoughts and feelings of discomfort behind your beliefs actually helps build healthier relationships.

Exercise on Testing Out Common Unhealthy Beliefs:

Belief:
"A partner should be by the side of their significant other at a social event, otherwise, it is not a good relationship."

Examining the Belief:

1. Who says that a partner should stick by their mate's side during a social event?
2. How realistic is that anyway?
3. What are my fears around my partner talking to his/her friends? Do I worry that my mate will find others more interesting or attractive? Do I feel others present at the event will judge that my relationship is a poor one?
4. Do I know of any healthy and loving relationships where the partners don't spend every moment glued to each other's sides at events?

Healthier ways to perceive the above example:

1. It is perfectly okay that my partner has her own friends.
2. I know she still loves me even when she is with friends or at an event or party.
3. It is healthy to have time apart at a party.

Determining Your Own Unhealthy Beliefs:

Write down what you believe is an unhealthy belief on the following line:

1. Core Belief:____
2. What percentage do you believe this belief is true? __________________%
3. List evidence that does *not* support this belief:

a ____

b____

c____

d____

e____

f ____

g____

h____

i____

j____

Now rewrite a healthier belief based on the evidence listed above:

1. New belief____
2. What percentage do you now believe this belief is true? __________%

CALL TO ACTION: Read this belief throughout the week. And reassess at the end of the week, and again at the end of the month. What percentage do you believe your revised belief to be true?

Defense Mechanisms

Defense mechanisms are common psychological coping strategies that help us deal with unwanted emotions and high levels of anxiety. They occur unconsciously, meaning we are unaware that we are utilizing them, which is why it is important to become aware of them, recognize how they show up and in what form, and how they impact our lives. While defense mechanisms may be useful in a crisis, such as an illness or natural disaster, continuing to avoid reality and distort the truth becomes a problem in itself when the original problem doesn't get handled.

Below is a list of defense mechanisms. They can be used independently or in combination with each other.

1. **Denial –** Denial is a defense against acknowledging and accepting a reality, such as the drug addiction of a loved-one, because facing the truth is unpleasant and painful. By denying the reality, one gets to avoid dealing with it. Denial, which can begin to show up in childhood, is one of the more primitive defense mechanisms.
   - *For example, an abuser will often deny they have a problem, pointing to the fact that their partner continues to stay with them.*

2. **Acting Out** – When someone shows their emotions through repeated or extreme behaviors (yelling or hitting) instead of expressing their thoughts and feelings more appropriately through verbal communication, it is referred to as "acting out." Someone who acts out probably doesn't trust that they will ever be heard if they *only* communicate verbally. They express their emotional pain physically which makes it more difficult for them to achieve the results they want. Typically when a person is acting out, they are not weighing the consequences of their actions.
   - *For example, instead of stating, "I'm feeling ignored," a person yells at their partner, uses profane language, and then leaves the room and slams the door.*

3. **Rationalization -** Rationalization is justifying and making excuses for one's actions instead of telling the truth about their motivation. It's explaining away one's behaviors and perceptions.
   a. *For instance, a man rationalizes hitting another man at a bar for looking at his girlfriend. In his mind, another man should never look at his girlfriend.*

4. **Displacement -** Displacement is the redirecting of pent-up feelings and impulses meant for *one* person or situation to *another* person who is less threatening and may have no actual involvement. People will use displacement when they feel it's not safe to express their anger at the person they are really mad at.
   - *For example: a woman gets upset at her manager, but because there's too much risk involved with showing anger in the workplace, she goes home and gets upset with her husband or children. Thus, she is redirecting her anger from her manager to her*

family. This creates additional problems: the original problem doesn't get resolved and now her husband and children have their own feelings to deal with.

5. **Projection** - Projection is when one person believes that another person has the thoughts and feelings that in reality they themselves have, but won't admit to (misattribution). This defense mechanism is utilized when an individual is embarrassed or ashamed of having such thoughts or feelings, so they project them onto somebody else.
   - *For example, a man may get upset because he thinks his wife wants to have an affair when he's really the one with the wandering eye.*

6. **Repression** - Repression is a defense mechanism that enables a person to block out unacceptable and painful thoughts and feelings, keeping them from consciousness, where they'd be intolerable to live with on a daily basis. The good news is that one can work through these painful memories with a professional therapist so the intensity of the memories diminishes and what triggers them can be understood and controlled.
   - *For example, a person may have experienced the trauma of childhood physical or sexual abuse from a parent or relative, but may have "forgotten" all about it in adulthood. They have repressed the painful memories so that they can continue to have a cordial and loving relationship with the abuser in the present.*

7. **Withdrawal** - Withdrawal is when one becomes passive and holds back something of value or interest from another. Though this is usually done unconsciously, it's a response to earlier emotional pain, so it's a way of protecting our vulnerability to that earlier pain and the unwanted emotions and thoughts that go along with it.
   - *For instance, a woman signals to her husband that she is interested in intimacy with him. When he doesn't respond, she feels rejected and withdraws from the relationship for the next week as a way to protect herself from this and earlier, painful rejections in her childhood. When he tries to hug her or talk to her, there's a sense of disconnect.*

8. **Dissociation** – Someone with a "dissociative reaction" to a painful earlier life event isolates that memory from ordinary consciousness so they can continue in the moment without the searing pain that memory would cause. They may lose track of their memory of the situation. One is most likely to dissociate if they have had a history of childhood trauma or abuse.
   - *For example, a man in a rage "sees red" and kills another man, but later on when he is arrested and asked what happened, he cannot recall the event.*

9. **Introjection –** Introjection has occurred when a person adopts someone else's values and opinions without exploring whether or not that standard suits or fits them. Often, a person *introjects* the values and morals of a judgmental parent, so that their own thoughts are now full of "*You should's*" and "*You should not's*." When a person relinquishes their own values and goes along with the values of others, it can result in unhappy personal relationships

later on in life because they are not being "themselves." Such people may be predisposed to acting out aggressively or passive aggressively.

- *For instance, in the workplace, one business partner keeps adapting to the other business partner's ideas even though he has good ideas of his own and does not necessarily agree with his partner. Eventually, he is bound to become resentful and act out his frustrations in ways that could put his partnership and business in jeopardy.*

10. **Undoing -** Undoing is when a person unconsciously tries to superficially repair a behavior or thought that was offensive or hurtful. This protects them from having to deal with the complex effects of the act.
    - *For instance, a woman suffering guilt from youthful sexual behavior now endlessly cleans her house ("Out, out damned spot!") without consciously connecting her cleaning to an attempt to "undo" the acts of the past.*

11. **Regression -** Regression is when a person re-adopts behavior from a less mature stage of life. This is done unconsciously, and usually when one is experiencing undesirable thoughts, feelings and stress.
    - *For example, a man has been waiting a while to be seated at a restaurant. He notices that people who arrived after him are being seated before him. This triggers unconscious associations to sibling rivalry in childhood. He instantly over-reacts, approaches the hostess with hostility and yells at her for attending to the needs of the other customers first.*

12. **Intellectualizing** - Intellectualization is when a person hides their true feelings about something and focuses on their beliefs or opinions instead.
    - *For example, a woman insists that it doesn't bother her when her boyfriend goes out to lunch with female co-workers, stating that it's his right, that the women are "just friends," and that she's "not the jealous type," but the truth is she's hurt, it makes her feel vulnerable, and she is angry at her boyfriend for needing to do this. Still, she uses logic-tight explanations for his behavior to keep herself, and him, from any awareness of how she really feels.*

Exercise

Step 1: Select the top three defense mechanisms that you use, and describe **how** you use them.

1. Type of Defense Mechanism:____

    a. How you use it: ____

    ____

    b. How it has impeded your growth: ____

    ____

    c. List a coping strategy or alternative action you could use in place of the defense mechanism in the future: ____

    ____

2. Type of Defense Mechanism:____

    a. How you use it: ____

    ____

    b. How it has impeded your growth: ____

    ____

    c. List a coping strategy or alternative action you could use in place of the defense mechanism in the future: ____

    ____

3. Type of Defense Mechanism:____

    1. How you use it: ____

    ____

    2. How it has impeded your growth: ____

    ____

    3. List a coping strategy or alternative action you could use in place of the defense mechanism in the future: ____

    ____

Ego and Anger

Ego is Born

When we first come into this world, our initial experiences involve our senses – our physical surroundings, sounds, smells, tastes, touch, and other people -- usually our mother, father, caregivers, and family members. A baby is sensitive to what's *outside* the self -- how others *feel* about him or her -- but is not yet aware of the "self." If others keep smiling at him or her, the baby feels appreciated -- and it is at this point that the "Ego," or the Center, is born. Our ego is further shaped and controlled by Society. If we behave a certain way, then Society appreciates us. If we don't, Society disapproves and our ego feels injured.

Let's take a look at some examples to demonstrate this point: The person behind you in the check-out line at the grocery store makes a comment that you're taking too long unloading your shopping cart. In reality, you haven't been physically harmed by the remark, but your "ego" feels the sting because your self-image is of someone who is organized and efficient and can unload a shopping cart quickly. So the remark makes you angry.

Ego and Anger are highly correlated.

A similar situation might involve dating. Say you see yourself as a pretty smooth operator in the dating world. You have an expectation that women will respond well to you. But then on your third date with a woman she tells you what she doesn't like about you, and she lists the reasons why she will not continue seeing you. Your expectation that she'll fall for you goes right out the window. You feel under attack. Your image of yourself as a smooth operator takes a big hit. You feel angry.

Again, *Ego and Anger are highly correlated.*

While it's easy to see how one's self-image and expectations can be threatened in these kinds of situations, the reality is that in neither situation has any real harm been done. Nothing has changed. Life is the same as it was. Still, we notice a *deep resistance* within ourselves and feel emotional distress. That's the ego at work, interfering with our ability to handle these situations with more grace. Too often what has happened is that a *present* event has triggered feelings from a *past* event, and for the moment we cannot differentiate between the two, or tell what's real and what's not real. That's why it's so important to learn all we can about the *ego* so we can better deal with it and save ourselves a lot of grief.

We Are Not Our Ego

The ego wants us to think that the ego is *us*, but it's really not. The ego is our *reflected being* but not our real self. The less we know about our real self, the more vulnerable we are to how others perceive us. If we perceive that no one likes us, appreciates us, or approves of us, then our ego is negatively impacted. We feel pain and rejection. We are hurt. But it doesn't have to be that way.

Resistance to Understanding Ego

When reality differs from our expectations and when we start experiencing negative emotions as the result of an ego blow, it's common to fall back on *resistance,* which only takes us away from the truth rather than towards it.

Resistance plays a role in our experience of pain and discomfort in several ways:

- We feel angry when our self-image is attacked or challenged.
- We feel betrayed when our significant other wants to date others.
- We experience anxiety when we worry that something may happen in the future that we don't want.
- We feel envious when others have something we think we should have.
- We experience loneliness when we don't have a significant person in our lives.
- We experience sadness when we want something that we can't have.

How to Deal with Our Ego?

It's difficult to see our own ego, yet so easy to see someone else's. The challenge is to see our own. The more we observe our own ego, the more capable we become of not letting it interfere. If we participate in any kind of self-reflective practice, such as mindful meditation, then we are probably already familiar with the concept of the ego. It's the little voice inside us that leads to worry, anxiety and suffering. It keeps us apart from the moment.

Think about your anxieties. It usually has to do with the future. "What if _______ happens?" But this future only exists within your mind, and nowhere else. You will deal with the situations as they arise, but you're not trusting that you can handle or manage them. Similar to anxiety being about the future, the ego also loves to keep us in the past. It rehashes the shame, guilt, and mistakes we've made. These could turn into obsessions. The goal is to *free ourselves from the ego* and be aware of the times that your ego gets in the way during an argument.

Exercise:

Questions to ask yourself when exploring your ego:

1- Did anything from my past upset me regarding this present situation?

____

2- Is my worry about the future impacting my current responses?

____

3- Do I worry that if I admit my responsibility for something that my partner will see me as a *weak* person?

____

4- Do I worry that by taking responsibility, it will set a precedent and from now on I'll be the one blamed?

____

5- Did what this person tell me interfere with how I perceive myself?

____

6- If I didn't have my ego to worry about, what would my responses be like?

____

7- If I were to come from a place of empathy and concern for my partner, how would I respond differently?

____

Why Forgiveness is Difficult

Forgiveness is hard. But why? Perhaps for the following reasons:

1. **We're often reluctant to let go of our anger**. One of the main reasons people get angry is to achieve or regain control. If we still feel harmed in the now—even years after we actually were—we frequently continue to feel angry. And it's inherently difficult, if not impossible, to forgive someone with whom we're still angry. This is true even if the predominant reason we're angry isn't due to frustration at having lost control but is due to outrage at the injustice committed against us (anger at injustice). But in the same way soft tissue inflammation is helpful only in the first few days after an injury occurs, often causing even more damage than the original injury if it's allowed to become chronic, anger—no matter what its cause—if allowed to boil without being harnessed to accomplish something worthwhile, can cause us far more harm than good.

2. **We want to satisfy our sense of justice**. Even if we're not angry, if we believe our offender doesn't deserve our forgiveness, we may find ourselves withholding it to avoid appearing to condone what they did to us.

3. **Forgiveness may feel like letting our offender off the hook without punishment**. Even if we don't feel that forgiveness implies we condone the injustice committed against us, to release our anger and forgive our offender may feel like letting them get away without being punished, especially if no other punishment is forthcoming.

4. **We wish to harm as we've been harmed**. An eye for an eye often feels viscerally satisfying. If we lack the power to deliver actual harm, harboring anger may feel like a second-best option. Holding a grudge does in a certain sense feel good.

5. **They haven't apologized**. The power of an apology to open the path to forgiveness can't be overestimated. Nor can the ability of withholding an apology—of the refusal to acknowledge a wrong was committed—to block it.

6. **When someone commits an injustice, we often cease to see or believe they could be capable of any good**. We tend to abstract those who harm us, diminishing them from full-fledged human beings into merely "our offenders." This enables us to refuse to allow into our conception of them any room for the possibility that they have positive characteristics or have the capability to do good (much in the same way they abstracted our full-fledged humanity into some label that enabled them to harm us in the first place).

What Does It Mean to Forgive?

Forgiveness involves recognizing that the person who harmed us is *more than just the person who harmed us*. He or she is in fact, whether we want to acknowledge it or not, a full-fledged human being whose full dimension isn't defined by their foolish decision to harm us in some way (as much as we may wish it were). At its core, forgiveness is an acknowledgment that a person who's harmed us still has the capacity for good.

Forgiveness requires us to view our offender not as malevolent but as confused—so much so that they would actually believe that by harming us they could somehow become happier (though they would almost certainly be incapable of articulating that as the reason). Secondly, forgiving requires us to let go—of our anger; of our desire to punish or teach a lesson; of our need to harm our harmer; of the notion that by choosing to forgive an offense we're in some way condoning an unjust action committed against us or committing an injustice ourselves; of the need for an apology; and of the need for our harmer to change. For in forgiving their transgression against us, we're ultimately seeking to *free ourselves*. Forgiving, as the saying also goes, doesn't mean forgetting. Nor does it have to mean returning the person we've forgiven to their former status in our lives. It means we move on healed from the hurt that's been done to us.

How Does Forgiving Others Benefit Us?

Forgiving others is the only way to break a cycle of violence (whether physical or otherwise).

In order to forgive, we must manifest a life-condition of compassion. In Nichiren Buddhism this is called the life-condition of the bodhisattva. A bodhisattva is someone whose most pressing concern lies with the happiness of others. Attaining this life-condition benefits no one more than it does us, as it is a life-condition of joy.

In order to forgive we must let go of our anger. If we continue to hold onto anger, it often leaks out against others who've committed no crime against us, as well as colors all our experiences, often ruining our ability to feel joy in many aspects of life.

Finding the Compassion to Forgive

In order to muster compassion for one who's harmed us, we must first believe with our lives that all people originally desire to become happy. From there we must find a way to realize our offender has simply gone completely awry in their pursuit of their own happiness and pity them as we would a misguided child. For no matter how sophisticated a person may seem, how confident and wise and successful, how could an intent to harm arise from anything other than a delusion?

The question will naturally arise: are some people's crimes so heinous that they don't merit forgiveness? Parents who've abused us? Children who've rebelled against us? Spouses who've abandoned us? Friends who've betrayed us? Strangers who've harmed us or our loved ones? Or even tyrants who've killed our families? Is Hitler, for example, forgivable? Can one forgive a person without forgiving their actions?

I would suggest only this: that if you find yourself holding onto a grudge against someone who's grievously harmed you, for you to find a way to forgive them—for you to *become* the kind of person who *can*—will not only first and foremost benefit you, but ultimately may have the power to transform the life of the person you're forgiving. Not always of course, but sometimes. And if it does, in forgiving them you're not only setting yourself free, you're actually contributing to something of greater importance, something the world is literally crying out for in more places than you could probably name: peace.

Appendix A

Pleasant Feelings

absorbed
accepting
admiration
admired
affected
affectionate
alive
amazed
animated
at ease
attracted
attractive
blessed
bold
brave
bright
calm
capable
centered
certain
challenged
cheerful
clever
close
comfortable
comforted
committed
compassionate
competent
concerned
confident
connected
considerate
content
courageous
curious
daring
dedicated
delighted
desired
determined
devoted
dynamic
eager
earnest
easy
ecstatic
elated
enchanted
encouraged
energetic
engrossed
enthusiastic
excited
exuberant
fascinated
festive
forgiving
fortunate
free
friendly
fulfilled
gay
generous
glad
gleeful
grateful
great
grounded
happy
heard
hopeful
important
impressed
independent
inquisitive
inspired
interested
intrigued
jolly
joyous
jubilant
keen
kind
liberated
liked
logical
loveable
loved
loving
lucky
merry
noticed
open
optimistic
overjoyed
pampered
passionate
peaceful
playful
pleased
positive
productive
quiet
reassured
receptive
recognized
refreshed
rejuvenated
relaxed
reliable
relieved
romantic
satisfied
secure
sense of belonging
sensitive
serene
significant
smart
soothed
spirited
stimulated
successful
sunny
supported
sure
surprised
sympathetic
sympathy
tenacious
tender
thankful
thrilled
touched
trusted
understanding
unique
valued
wanted
warm
warmhearted
whole
worthy
youthful

Unpleasant and Difficult Feelings

abandoned
accused
afflicted
aggravated
aggressive
agitated
agonized
alarmed
alienated
alone
ambushed
anguish
annoyed
anxious
appalled
ashamed
attacked
awkward
bad
belittled
belligerent
betrayed
bitter
blamed
blue
boiling
bored
broken
bummed
burdened
burned-out
cheated
churning
cold
confused
controlled
cornered
cranky
crushed
deceived
defensive
dejected
dependent
depressed
deprived
despair
despair
desperate
despicable
detestable
diminished
disappointed
disconnected
discouraged
disgusting
disillusioned
disinterested
dismayed
disrespected
dissatisfied
distressed
distrustful
dominated
doubtful
dull
embarrassed
empty
enraged
excluded
exploited
exposed
fatigued
fearful
forced
frightened
frustrated
fuming
furious
grief
grouchy
guarded
guilty
hateful
heartbroken
helpless
hesitant
hopeless
hostile
humiliated
hurt
Ill-tempered
impatient
impulsive
inadequate
incapable
incensed
indecisive
indifferent
indignant
inferior
inflamed
infuriated
injured
insensitive
insulted
interrogated
irate
irked
irritable
irritated
isolated
jealous
judged
livid
lonely
lost
lousy
mad
malicious
manipulated
miffed
miserable
misgiving
mistreated
misunderstood
mocked
mournful
needy
nervous
nonchalant
nosy
numb
offended
offensive
out of control
outraged
overwhelmed
pained
panic
paralyzed
peeved
perplexed
perturbed
pessimistic
pissed off
powerless
preoccupied
provocative
provoked
rage
raving
rebellious
reckless
rejected
repugnant
resentful
reserved
restless
revengeful
riled up

sad
scared
seething
sense of loss
shaky
shy
skeptical
sore
sorrowful
spiteful
steamed
stupefied
suffocated
sulky
suspicious
tearful
tense
terrible
terrified
threatened
ticked off
timid
tormented
tortured
tragic
trapped
unappreciated
uncertain
uncomfortable
undesired
uneasy
unhappy
unloved
unmotivated
unpleasant
unsupported
unsure
unworthy
upset
uptight
used
useless
vengeful
vexed
victimized
violent
volatile
vulnerable
weary
woeful
worked up
worried
wronged

Resources

Books

Burns, D., M.D. (1990; 1999). *The Feeling Good Handbook*. The Penguin Group.

Cohen-Posey, K. (2000), *Brief Therapy Client Handouts.* Wiley Publishers.

Davis, M., Ph.D., Paleg, K., Ph.D. & Fanning, P. (2004). *The Messages Workbook*. New Harbinger Publications.

Eifert, G. H., Forsyth, J.P., Hayes, S.C., & McKay, M. (2006), *ACT on Life Not on Anger: The New Acceptance & Commitment Therapy Guide to Problem Anger.* New Harbinger Publications.

Greenberger , D., & Padesky, C. (1995). *Mind Over Mood: Change How You Feel by Changing the Way You Think*. The Guildford Press.

Johnson, S. L. (1997; 2004), *The Therapist's Guide to Clinical Intervention: The 123's of Treatment Planning.* Academic Press, San Diego.

Lickerman, A., M.D., (2012). *The Undefeated Mind on the Science of Constructing an Indestructible Self*. Health Communications. Deerfield Beach, Florida.

Mallody, P., Miller, A.W., Miller, J.K., (1989; 2003) *Facing Codependence: What it Is, Where it Comes from, How it Sabotages our Lives.* HarperCollins, San Francisco.

Mellody, P., & Freundlich, L.S., (2003). *The Intimacy Factor: The Ground Rules for Overcoming the Obstacles to Truth, Respect, and Lasting Love.* HarperSanFrancisco.

Potter, R.T., MSW, PhD. (2005), *Handbook of Anger Management: Individual, Couple, Family, and Group Approaches*. The Haworth Clinical Practice Press; The Haworth Reference Press; and imprints of The Haworth Press, Inc.

Schiraldi, G. R., Ph.D., & Kerr, M.H., Ph.D. (2002). *The Anger Management Sourcebook*. McGraw Hill.

Journal Articles

Ellis, A. (1991). The revised ABC's of rational-emotive therapy (RET), *Journal of Rational-Emotive and Cognitive-Behavior Therapy*, Volume 9, Number 3, Page 139.

Lund, R. (2014). Stressful social relations and mortality: a prospective cohort study, *The Journal of Epidemiology and Community Health*, doi:10.1136/jech-2013-203675.

Miller, R. (2013). Marital Quality and Health Over 20 Years: A Growth Curve Analysis, *Journal of Marriage and Family,* 75:3 (June 2013), pp. 667–680; doi: 10.1111/jomf.12025.

Pickering, M., Communication in explorations, *A Journal of Research of the University of Maine,* Vol. 3, No. 1, Fall 1986, pp 16-19.

Platt, Jim, *Crossing the Line: Anger vs. Rage,* Working@Dartmouth, http://74.125.95.104/search?q=cache:PviYnlwDmTAJ:www.dartmouth.edu/~hrs/pdfs

Sanford, K, (2010). Perceived Threat and Perceived Neglect: Couples' Underlying Concerns During Conflict, *Psychological Assessment, American Psychological Association,* Vol. 22, No. 2, pp. 288-297.

Smith, P. N., & Ziegler, D. J. (2004) Anger and the ABC model underlying Rational-Emotive Therapy, *Psychological Reports*, Vol. 94, pp. 1009-1014.

Sturmey, Peter. *Cognitive therapy with people with intellectual disabilities: A selective review and critique.* Clinical Psychology & Psychotherapy11.4 (2004): 222-232

Blogs and Online Resources

15 Common Defense Mechanisms. *Psych Central.* http://psychcentral.com/lib/15-common-defense-mechanisms/0001251

Active Listening Skills. AGING I&R/A TIPS. *Tip Sheet 1*. National Aging Information & Referral Support Center.
http://www.nasuad.org/documentation/I_R/ActiveListening.pdf

Lickerman, A., M.D. (2012) *The Undefeated Mind: On the Science of Constructing an Indestructible Self.* Health Communications & http://www.happinessinthisworld.com

Mills, H., Ph.D., *Physiology of Anger*.
http://www.mhcinc.org/poc/view_doc.php?type=doc&id=5805&cn=116

Osho. *Ego - The False Center*. Beyond the Frontier of the Mind.
http://deoxy.org/egofalse.htm

Patterson, K. & Grenny, J. (2006). *Unresponsive Spouse*.
http://www.crucialskills.com/2006/04/

Platt, Jim, *Crossing the Line: Anger vs. Rage,*
Working@Dartmouth, http://74.125.95.104/search?q=cache:PviYnlwDmTAJ:www.dartmouth.edu/~hrs/pdfs

Shaadi.com and IMRB(2012). Survey: Couples Who Argue Together Stay Together, http://imrbint.com/downloads/Shaadi.com%20-%20IMRB%20International%20Report_FINAL_Latest.pdf

Vivyan, C. (2010). *What are My Options?*
www.getselfhelp.co.uk

Websites

http://imperial.networkofcare.org/mh/
(http://imperial.networkofcare.org/mh/library/article.aspx?id=367)
http://www.mayoclinic.org/healthy-living/adult-health/in-depth/anger-management/art-20045434

About the Author

Author *Anita Avedian* is a Licensed Marriage and Family Therapist practicing in Beverly Hills, Tarzana, Sherman Oaks and Glendale, California. She graduated with her M.S. in Educational Psychology and completed two certifications including Employee Assistance Program and Human Resources from California State University of Northridge. Her specialties include working with relationships, anger, anxiety, and addictions. Anita is the Director of Anger Management 818, helping both self-referred and court-ordered individuals seek help with their aggression. She has six Centers in the Greater Los Angeles area covering various anger management programs. Anita has authored this program with the help of her staff. Anita Avedian is a National Anger Management Association (NAMA) authorized trainer and supervisor, and offers a certification program to those interested in offering anger management services.

Anita is very involved with the professional community. She is the co-founder of the California Association of Anger Management Providers, which is currently the California Chapter of NAMA. Anita is the Founder of Toastmasters for Mental Health Professionals, and serves on the Board for the Armenian American Mental Health Association, the San Fernando Valley Chapter of Employee Assistance Professional Association, and she served on the San Fernando Valley Chapter of the California Association of Marriage and Family Therapists for many years.

57144903R00082

Made in the USA
Middletown, DE
28 July 2019